Second Language Pedagogy

N. S. Prabhu

Oxford University Press
1987

Oxford University Press, Walton Street, Oxford OX2 6DP
Oxford New York Toronto
Delhi Bombay Calcutta Madras Karachi
Petaling Jaya Singapore Hong Kong Tokyo
Nairobi Dar es Salaam Cape Town
Melbourne Auckland
and associated companies in
Beirut Berlin Ibadan Nicosia

OXFORD is a trade mark of Oxford University Press

ISBN 0 19 437084 4

The author and publishers would like to thank the following for
permission to reproduce the material below:

Alan Beretta and Alan Davies for the article 'Evaluation of the
Bangalore Project' (copyright Oxford University Press) (Appendix VI).

The British Council for the unpublished report 'Procedures in teaching
the structures "the green line is very long, the white one is very short"'
by S. Durairaj (Appendix 1b).

A Gilpin and B. Kumaravadivelu, and Esther Ramani, for the lesson
transcripts (Appendix VI).

The Indian Express for the article 'Learning English Without Tears'
(Appendix 1a).

The Regional Institute of English (Bangalore) for the extracts from
RIE Bulletin, Special Series No. 2, and RIE Newsletters 1/1 and 1/2
(Appendix II).

The Regional Language Centre (Singapore) of the Southeast Asian
Ministers of Education Organization for the extract from N.S. Prabhu:
'The teaching of English and notions about communication'
(Appendix II).

Set by Hope Services, Abingdon
Printed in Hong Kong

P51
P72
1987

Contents

Appendices

Acknowledgements

I wish to acknowledge my deep sense of indebtedness to the following:

The Regional Institute of English, Bangalore (in particular, V. C. Devasundaram, its director at the time) for providing initial sponsorship and support to the Communicational Teaching Project.

The British Council, for enabling me to work on the project and for providing support in a number of ways.

The teachers and specialists who joined the project team at various times and contributed generously of their time and thought. They are: A. Arulpragasam, K. Subrahmanya Bhat, M. N. K. Bose, David Carroll, S. Damodaran, Sister M. Eleanora, T. Elia, Francis Jayachandran, Geoffrey Kaye, I. S. Nagaraja, Lalitha Obed, C. Radha, Esther Ramani, S. Renganayaki, T. R. Keshava Rao, V. Saraswathi, R. Vadivelu and Vanamala Vishwanatha.

The many applied linguists who took an interest in the project, helped to further my thinking through discussion, and gave me valuable advice and support. Among them are: Dick Allwright, Robert Bellarmine, Alan Beretta, Christopher Brumfit, Alan Davies, Arlene Gilpin, A. P. R. Howatt, Keith Johnson, B. Kumaravadivelu, Yasmeen Lukmani, Maria Pavesi, R. Shanthakumari, H. G. Widdowson, and Regina Winert.

The Charles Wallace India Trust, the Hornby Trust, and Oxford University Press for financial assistance in writing this book.

The University of Edinburgh for providing me with facilities for doing the writing.

N.S.P.

1   The Context

This book aims to present a particular view of second language pedagogy, together with an account of a five-year project of exploratory teaching which helped to articulate that view and to develop procedures of teaching consistent with it.[1]

The project consisted of teaching English to a small number of classes in primary and secondary schools in southern India, over periods of time varying between one and three years. The teaching was planned, carried out, and reviewed regularly by a group of interested teacher trainers and teachers of English as a part-time activity, but with institutional support from the Regional Institute of English in Bangalore and the British Council in Madras. Some comments which have appeared in the literature refer to the project as the 'Bangalore Project', the 'Bangalore-Madras Project', or the 'Procedural Syllabus Project', but the project team itself used the name 'Communicational Teaching Project'.[2]

The stimulus for the project was a strongly-felt pedagogic intuition, arising from experience generally but made concrete in the course of professional debate in India. This was that the development of competence in a second language requires not systematization of language inputs or maximization of planned practice, but rather the creation of conditions in which learners engage in an effort to cope with communication.[3] This view will be discussed at some length in later chapters of the book, but one or two points can be made at this stage to prevent possible misunderstanding. In the context of the project, competence in a language was seen as consisting primarily of an ability to conform automatically to grammatical norms, and communication as a matter of understanding, arriving at, or conveying meaning. The focus of the project was not, that is to say, on 'communicative competence' (in the restricted sense of achieving social or situational appropriacy, as distinct from grammatical conformity) but rather on grammatical competence itself, which was hypothesized to develop in the course of meaning-focused activity.[4] Attempts to systematize inputs to the learner through a linguistically organized syllabus, or to maximize the practice of particular parts of language structure through activities deliberately planned for that purpose were regarded as being unhelpful to the development of grammatical competence and detrimental to the desired preoccupation with meaning in the classroom. Both the development and the exercise of grammatical competence were viewed as internal self-regulating processes and, furthermore, effort to exercise competence in response to a need to arrive at or convey meaning was viewed as a favourable condition for its development. It was decided that teaching should consequently be concerned with creating conditions for coping with meaning in the classroom, to the exclusion of any deliberate regulation of the development of grammatical competence or a mere simulation of language behaviour.[5]

The teaching which was undertaken was exploratory in three ways. First, it was an attempt to develop in the course of sustained teaching in actual classrooms, and by trial and error, a teaching methodology which was consistent with the initial intuition and maximally replicable in relation to such classrooms. The methodology which developed has since been referred to as 'task-based teaching' and will be discussed in this book in some detail. Secondly, the teaching was a means of developing a clearer perception of the intuition and of articulating it more fully in a number of ways. As the perception was influenced by the teaching, the teaching too was influenced by the emerging perception, so that theory and practice helped to develop each other in the course of the five years. Thirdly, the process of this development was reported as fully and frequently as possible to a wide audience of teachers and specialists in India, through periodical newsletters and at annual review seminars, in an effort to expose it as fully as possible to fellow-teachers' criticism or corroboration at every stage.[6] The regular debate thus generated, not only with teachers and specialists in India but, to a significant extent, with visiting specialists from outside India, was an important input to the project.[7] It is possible to think of progress in pedagogy as resulting from a continual interaction not only between perception and practice but also between differing perceptions, so that focused debate becomes a valuable means of sharing and influencing perceptions in ways that act as a process of error elimination. It is in this spirit that the project was submitted for discussion in India at various stages and it is in the same spirit that it is now being submitted for wider discussion.

It will be clear from the above that the project was not designed as an experiment to 'prove' a given methodology empirically, but was rather a classroom operation for developing a methodology and gaining some understanding of it.[8] An attempt was, however, made to see to what extent empirical evidence of outcomes can be obtained within the constraints of such an exercise and the result is included as Appendix VI. Equally, it has not been possible, with the staffing support available to the project, to gather and analyse observational data from the classroom as extensively or systematically as might have been desirable, though readers will, I hope, be able to form an impression of what teaching on the project was like from the description in the next chapter and the lesson transcripts in Appendix IV.[9] In general, what is offered in this book is an interpretation of classroom experience, with as clear an indication as possible of both the nature of the experience and the point of view from which the interpretation is made. Perhaps this will, among other things, serve to illustrate the value or otherwise of a project of this kind.

The project's concern for developing teaching procedures which are realistic and replicable in the Indian classroom does not necessarily imply that these procedures are being recommended for large-scale implementation in India. Nor does it imply that the relevance of such procedures is limited to Indian conditions. There can be different views on the relationship between pedagogic innovation and large-scale implementation, and my own is outlined in the last chapter of this book. On the question of local and global relevance, while it is true that teaching and learning situations can vary to a large extent on one or more of several dimensions, it would be unfortunate if innovations related to real and specific situations were, for that reason, assumed to be of limited relevance; one consequence of such an assumption might be to place too high a value, in terms of range of relevance, on innovation based on abstraction or idealization.[10] A more desirable course would be to assume that an innovation has relevance beyond the specific situation it is associated with and to examine, for any given situation, at what level of generality such relevance can be established. This would involve asking questions of the form 'Why not?' rather than 'Why?' and seeking to eliminate application at too low a level of generality. Relating specific dimensions of a situation to particular aspects of a pedagogic proposal in this way can in itself be a fruitful activity. Typologies of teaching situations – commonly made in terms such as 'second' and 'foreign' languages, 'elementary', 'intermediate' and 'advanced' levels, 'young' and 'adult' learners – should thus be seen as an aid to investigating the extent of relevance of a pedagogic proposal, not as a means of treating pedagogic proposals as merely pragmatic responses to specific situations.

This is not to deny that features of specific teaching situations influence the feasibility of particular pedagogic procedures and, indeed, the development of particular pedagogic perceptions. An important feature of the English-teaching situation in India is that English is a part of statutory 'mainstream' education, with such factors as the allocation of time, the size of classes, and examination requirements decided on in the context of the teaching of all other subjects. Second language teaching in this institutional context has to come to terms with the norms and expectations of formal education in general. There are, for instance, perceptions of the roles of teachers and learners in the classroom and there is an expectation of serious, substantive content to handle. When pedagogic perceptions of language as skill or of language learning as a matter of social interaction lead to classroom activities such as playing games or acting out non-classroom roles, 'having fun' or managing without the teacher, there is a conflict with the norms of formal education and with what may be called the 'classroom ethos'.[11] The traditional perception of language as formal grammar, and of language learning as a matter of studying (or translating or memorizing) serious texts, suited the educational framework much better. This is not to suggest that the constraints of formal education should have precedence over innovative perceptions of language pedagogy; but neither should it be assumed that these perceptions can, or should necessarily seek to, alter the formal context of teaching. Developing feasible classroom procedures based on a given perception of pedagogy involves a reconciliation with the constraints of the teaching context, and it should be regarded as a strength for classroom procedures to be able to develop within and draw support from such constraints while remaining consistent with the perception involved. It is one of the advantages of a teaching project which is not a 'designed experiment' that it is able to explore the possibilities of such reconciliation and ensure some general viability to the teaching procedures it develops. Thus, while the pedagogic perception behind the project in southern India is that language ability develops in direct relation to communicational effort (and that language structure as content is unhelpful in language teaching), the teaching procedures which evolved on the project crucially involve a preoccupation with meaning-content and activities in which teachers act as teachers and learners act as learners in the way they do in the rest of the school's work. It will be claimed that both the focus on meaning-content and teacher-directed activity are advantages from the point of view of the perception of learning in question.[12]

It may be useful to conclude this discussion by mentioning some general features of the English-teaching situation in India. English has the constitutional status of an 'associate official language' in a highly multilingual national context and is the dominant medium of higher-level administration, higher education, the learned professions, large-scale industry and commerce, and a considerable part of literary and artistic activity. Indians who use English are estimated to constitute only about 5 per cent of the nation's population, but this group forms a very large proportion of those who are in leadership roles and are concentrated in the largest cities in the country, where English functions as a lingua franca. The age at which the teaching of English starts at school varies between different states, but is generally between 7 and 12 years. Examinations in English at school-leaving and first-degree stages are compulsory in the majority of states and optional in others. Only a small proportion of the students being taught English at school, those in the large cities and from highly-educated or high-income backgrounds, come into contact with the language outside the language classroom. This may be in subject classes in the small number of private English-medium schools, or at home. English is, however, widely regarded by students and parents alike as the language of opportunity, opening the door to higher education, a better job, upward social mobility, and so on. Consequently, there is a widespread general desire to learn the language. An estimate of the number of students being taught English throughout the country at this time is twenty million, and virtually all the teachers of English are Indians who have learnt English in the same educational system. Class size in primary schools varies from 30 to 45 and in secondary schools from 40 to 60. Few classes use teaching aids beyond the blackboard, chalk, paper, and pencil.

Notes

1 No distinction is made here between 'second' and 'foreign' languages. Some indication of the teaching situation which gave rise to the project can be found later in this chapter and in the next.

2 See Johnson (1982: 135–44); Brumfit (1984a: 101–9); Brumfit

(1984b: 233–41); Howatt (1984: 288); Beretta and Davies (1985: 121–7).

3 There is a parallel to this in Brumfit's account of how he was led to formulate the principle of fluency activity in language teaching (1984a: 50–51).

4 The view developed during the course of the project thus differs from what is generally called 'communicative language teaching' both with regard to objectives (grammatical competence in the former case, a distinct communicative competence in the latter) and with regard to means (meaning focused activity in the former case, practice activity organized in terms of features' of situational appropriacy in the latter). This point will be taken up again in the next chapter.

5 The project group became aware with the publication of Krashen (1981), when the project had completed two years, of the striking similarity between these concepts and Krashen's concepts of 'acquisition' and 'comprehensible input'. There are, however, significant differences which will become clear at various points later on.

The general concept of second language acquisition as an internal, self-regulating process is, of course, an old one. Howatt points out how, as long ago as 1622 (in the context of teaching Latin), Joseph Webbe had argued that 'no man can run speedily to the mark of language that is shackled and ingiv'd with grammar precepts' and 'By exercise of reading, writing, and speaking after ancient Custom . . . all things belonging to Grammar will without labour, and whether we will or no, thrust themselves upon us' (1984: 34–5; and also 192–208 for a survey of other such proposals through the ages). Similarly, Palmer argued that (1) 'in learning a second language, we learn without knowing what we are learning', (2) 'the utilization of [the adult learner's] conscious and focused attention [on language] militates against the proper functioning of the natural capacities of assimilation', and (3) in teaching a second language 'we must design forms of work in which the student's attention shall be directed towards the subject matter and away from the form in which it is expressed' (1921: 44, 8, 51). Bloomfield thought too, that 'our fundamental mistake has been to regard language teaching as the imparting of a set of facts. . . . Language is not a process of logical reference to a conscious set of rules; the process of understanding, speaking, and writing is everywhere an associative one. Real language teaching consists, therefore, of building up in the pupil those associative habits which constitute the language to be learned' (1914: 294). These are arguments against the overt teaching of grammar: the project has been concerned with developing an alternative to covert grammatical systematization as well, as will be seen in later chapters.

6 The Newsletters were published as a Special Series by the Regional Institute of English in Bangalore and consist of 1/1 (July 1979), 1/2 (September 1979), 1/3 (March 1980), 1/4 (April 1980), 2/1 (October 1980), and 2/2 (October 1980). Mimeographed lesson reports continued to be made available from the British Council office in Madras, from October 1980 to February 1982. Teaching in the last two years of the project (1982–4) was based largely on a re-use of classroom tasks devised earlier, with new classes, in different schools, and by different teachers.

The introduction to the first Newsletter said: 'We are publishing [these reports] in an attempt to share with interested fellow-professionals our thoughts on a possible new direction for English language teaching in India. . . . It is common for those who innovate to concentrate on defending or disseminating what they advocate. This series is an attempt to record, at every stage, our assumptions, methods, doubts and conclusions so that those who wish to may examine them; in this way the weaknesses, which we assume are many, may be discovered before they do much damage – or we ourselves are tempted to cover them up! Furthermore, we hope that, as the project develops, a body of theory about how one can employ a communicational approach in the teaching of English to school-age learners will be evolved; for this reason, the records of the lessons, which are the breeding ground of new theory, are included in some detail with the conclusions that arose from the group's discussion of these lessons as it observed them.'

7 The visiting specialists who participated in different review seminars are: Keith Johnson, Dick Allwright, Christopher Brumfit, Douglas Barnes, S. Pit Corder and Alan Davies. In addition, Keith Johnson and Henry Widdowson participated in two earlier seminars which prepared the ground for the project.

8   Richards (1984: 19–20) criticizes the project for not being a 'true experiment' and concludes that, for that reason, little can be learnt from its results. While the account given in this book might enable the reader to judge what value there is to a project which is not a 'true' experiment, it is also possible to ask how realistic it is to expect progress in language pedagogy from 'true' experiments. Brumfit provides fundamental arguments for the view that 'it makes little sense to treat language teaching, or indeed any teaching, as if it can be prescribed as a result of experimentation or predictive hypothesizing at a specific level' (1984a: 21). See also Ericson and Ellett (1982: 506): 'Our coin of knowledge is not firm generalizations, but is more akin to the good measure of meanings: plausibility. In educational research, as in education as a whole, good judgement should be seen as the prized intellectual capacity. Good judgement will not yield certainty, but it can yield interpretations and analyses far more acute and powerful than even the most skilful application of the empiricist "scientific method".'

More specifically, experimentation in language teaching seems to me to face three major problems: (1) the measurement of language competence involves elicitation (in some form) of specific language behaviour, but the relationship between such elicited behaviour and language competence which manifests itself in natural use is unclear; (2) given the view that the development of linguistic competence is a holistic process, there is not enough knowledge available either to identify and assess different intermediate stages of that development or to relate those stages to some table of norms which can be said to represent expectations, and (3) there is, ultimately, no way of attributing, with any certainty, any specific piece of learning to any specific teaching: language learning can take place independently of teaching intentions and it is impossible to tell what has been learnt because of some teaching, and what in spite of it.

9   Collingham (1981), Gilpin (1981), Kumaravadivelu (1981), and Mizon (1981), all provide further samples and analyses of classroom discourse on the project. See also Rajan (1983) and Saraswathi (1984).

10   Brumfit (1984a: 17–18) provides a concise statement of the various dimensions of situational variation.

11 See Howatt (1984: 297): 'The exchange of ideational meanings is more amenable to the conditions of the typical classroom than interpersonal socialization (particularly if it is role-played or simulated).'

12 There is perhaps an informative comparison to make between innovations in second language teaching arising in contexts of formal education, and those with their origins in special functional texts (e.g. the Berlitz Schools, the Army Specialized Training Program in the USA, present-day pre-sessional language courses, and private language schools). The comparison may suggest relationships between types of teaching contexts and forms of innovation on the one hand, and the limits (and effects) of generalization across contexts on the other.

2 The Project

The purpose of this chapter is to provide a factual account of the project, confining attention to what was thought and done at different points in its development and leaving a more detailed discussion of the issues involved to later chapters. It should therefore be seen as a historical description rather than an interpretation or justification. I will first indicate how the initial pedagogic perception took shape and then describe aspects of the teaching that was done.

Background

The Structural-Oral-Situational method

It is relevant to look briefly at the theory of English language teaching which has been prevalent in India in the past thirty years and which formed the background to the project's initial perception. A major innovation in teaching English was introduced into the state education system between 1955 and 1965, at the initiative of the state and central governments and with substantial assistance from abroad. The innovation consisted, essentially, of the use of structurally and lexically graded syllabuses, situational presentation of all new teaching items, balanced attention to the four language skills (but with listening and speaking preceding reading and writing), and a great deal of controlled practice using techniques such as the substitution table and choral repetition.[1] This was in contrast to earlier procedures such as the translation and explication of written texts, the reading aloud and memorization of texts, and a good deal of explicit grammar in the form of sentence analysis and parsing. Large programmes for the intensive re-training of teachers were conducted to implement the innovation, and ten state-level institutions were established in different parts of the country to provide more systematic and continual in-service teacher training and to create support services such as the provision of textbooks, teachers' guides, and radio broadcasts. In addition, a large national institution was set up to provide specialist-level training to potential teacher trainers and to undertake research-level activity in support of the teaching reform.

The Regional Institute of English in Bangalore was one of the ten state-level institutions, set up in 1963, to serve southern India following a massive 'campaign' of intensive teacher re-training based in Madras between 1959 and 1963.[2] This institute has used the term 'S-O-S' (Structural-Oral-Situational) to refer to the pedagogic principles it has been helping to implement and I shall be using that term, for convenience, at various points in this book. The indication given above of what the principles consisted of is perhaps an over-simplification, but two of the appendices to this book will help to show how the innovation was viewed at the time of its implementation. Appendix Ia reproduces a report which appeared in 1960 in a popular Indian newspaper, and which indicates not only what a demonstration of the new method was like but how there was a general sense of excitement about its potential. Appendix Ib is a form of assessment, made in 1965, of observable effects in the classroom of the 1959–63 'campaign' in Madras.

By about 1975, S-O-S was being regarded as a well-established method of teaching English, though there was some doubt about how well it had been transmitted to teachers and how widely its procedures were actually being followed in the numerous classrooms. S-O-S principles were, at the same time, increasingly being questioned, mainly on the grounds that learners' ability to make correct sentences in a classroom-practice situation did not ensure that they could make sentences correctly in other contexts, and that, although learners seemed to learn each structure well at the time it was taught, their command of language structure at the end of a structurally graded course lasting several years was still very unsatisfactory, requiring a good deal of remedial re-teaching which, in turn, led to similarly unsatisfactory results. It was also being suggested that concentration in the classroom on one structural pattern at a time might be inducing an overgeneralization of particular structural patterns leading to an increase in errors, and that the attempt to achieve comparable progress in all four language skills might be resulting in a holding back of attainable progress in the important receptive skill of reading. In addition, it was felt that the requirement of varied oral situational presentation of each new teaching item made too high a demand on teachers' inventiveness, while structural and lexical grading led to an artificial and dull repititiousness both in textbook materials and in classroom activity. There was, however, no clear evidence that learners' attainment levels were higher or lower than they had been under an earlier method of teaching, and it is therefore possible that the discontent being expressed largely represented a wearing out of the intellectual momentum of S-O-S pedagogy and a loss of plausibility to some of the perceptions behind it. This discontent was reinforced by an awareness of new pedagogic approaches being explored abroad – such as notional/functional syllabuses, communicative perspectives on language, and the designing of specific-purpose courses. As a result, a series of professional seminars were held in different parts of the country for the purpose of discussing one or another of the new approaches.

Preparatory discussion

Two such seminars were held at the Regional Institute of English in Bangalore. Participants included the specialist staff of both the Regional Institute itself and several of its sister institutions, English language specialists from some universities and state education departments, specialist staff of the British Council in India, and a visiting specialist at each seminar from a British University. At the first seminar held in January 1978, the discussion focused on notional/functional syllabuses (as proposed in Wilkins 1976 and presented at that seminar by Keith Johnson), while the second seminar focused on a discourse view of language and its pedagogic implications (as put forward in Widdowson 1978 and presented at the seminar by Henry Widdowson himself).[3]

It is natural for discussion at such seminars to be interpreted and responded to differently by different participants: what follows is my own view of how that discussion related to the project. Although the two seminars examined two different approaches to second language pedagogy, they threw up very similar problems for local participants in relating those approaches to their own situation and perceptions. The difficulty can perhaps be stated in the form of three conceptual mismatches.

First, an important principle of the prevailing S-O-S pedagogy was that grammar in the classroom was to be only implicit, not explicit – that is to say, grammar was to be used only for systematizing language data and for organizing practice materials, not for providing learners with an explicit knowledge of the rules. Explicit grammar in the classroom would only lead to a knowledge *about* the language, not an ability to make correct sentences automatically – a point forcefully argued by Palmer (1921), whose insight lay behind the structural syllabus and the associated procedures of situational presentation and practice. His point was that learners would internalize structural patterns subconsciously and, as a result, be able to employ them automatically if they encountered sets of sentences exemplifying particular structural patterns under conditions which ensured that they understood the meaning of the sentences concerned.[4] Influenced by Palmer's thinking, S-O-S pedagogy had aimed to promote in learners an internal grammatical competence which would manifest itself in the natural use of grammatically correct language. Although there was now a good deal of discontent being felt about that pedagogy, an internal grammatical competence was still seen by many participants in the seminars to be the main objective of language teaching. However, the new approaches based themselves on the argument that natural language use involved much more than a grammatical competence (which was persuasive enough), and that language pedagogy should therefore address itself to those additional forms of competence (which was much less persuasive). If one granted that there were dimensions to language use distinct from grammatical competence, it did not necessarily follow that these additional dimensions were more important for pedagogy than grammatical competence and should be paid attention to at its expense. The issue of how grammatical competence itself is best developed in learners did not seem to be addressed by the new proposals being examined. Examples of how grammatically correct sentences could still be socially inappropriate were not very helpful while available forms of pedagogy were found to be inadequate for enabling learners to achieve grammatical correctness itself, and social appropriacy did not seem a particularly pressing objective for second language learners in a formal educational setting.

Secondly, proposals for communicative teaching seemed to aim at an activation or extension of the grammatical competence already acquired by learners, for real-life use in particular areas of activity such as social discourse or academic study. It followed that courses constructed for such teaching were limited-purpose ones meant for learners already at an intermediate or advanced level of grammatical competence and were not significantly concerned with developing that competence itself.[5] The search in southern India, however, was for procedures of teaching suitable for schoolchildren and capable of developing grammatical competence from early stages.

Thirdly, it was true that notional syllabuses had been proposed (in the context of the Council of Europe's work)[6] for the early stages of language learning and that one of the arguments for using such semantic syllabuses was, attractively, that they would increase attention to meaning in the classroom and make the learning of the grammatical system less conscious.[7] However, such syllabuses did envisage a matching of each notional category with one or more linguistic forms, which meant that in the classroom the linguistic forms concerned were to be presented and practised in situations suggested by the notional category. It was not clear that this was significantly different, in terms of what happens in the classroom, from the situational presentation of language items from a linguistically organized syllabus. There was an inevitable loss of grammatical systematicity, while such semantic systematicity as was attainable seemed to have more value for a European context (in bringing about some comparability between courses in different languages) than for places like India. More importantly, the replacement of one mode of syllabus organization by another did not entail any major difference, in terms of classroom activity, from S-O-S pedagogy: specific items of language would still be pre-selected for any teaching unit and practised in contexts which suited them.

In general, the development of grammatical competence in learners continued to be viewed as the primary objective (and problem) in teaching English in India, while communicative approaches were seen to be concerned generally with objectives other than grammatical competence.

Initial perception

At the two seminars, discussion arising from such differing perceptions helped to heighten an awareness of the issues involved and, in particular, led to a re-examination of the assumptions of S-O-S pedagogy. The reason why grammar was to be used only for organizing the samples of language to be presented to learners was that learners would thereby be led to abstract the relevant structural patterns directly from the samples and at a subconscious level of the mind – 'we learn without knowing what we are learning' (Palmer 1921: 44). It was this subconscious abstraction of the grammatical system that enabled the system to operate subconsciously in learners' later language use in a way that knowledge resulting from explicit grammar teaching would not operate – 'We form our sentences in unconscious obedience to some rules unknown to us' (Palmer 1921: 5). The issue was thus one of the nature of grammatical knowledge to be developed: if the desired form of knowledge was such that it could *operate* subconsciously, it was best for it to *develop* subconsciously as well. S-O-S pedagogy attempted to regulate and facilitate the process by which learners abstracted the grammatical system by (1) ordering the elements of the system in ways considered to be helpful for learning, (2) limiting the samples of language presented to learners in such a way that only one new element had to be abstracted at a time, and (3) increasing the chances of the new element being abstracted by increasing the number of relevant samples encountered by learners – devices which may be called (1) planned progression, (2)ʼ pre-selection, and (3) form-focused activity. The use of these devices, it was hoped, would not alter the nature of the knowledge they were trying to promote. However, in re-examining that assumption, and in reviewing actual experience of such teaching, it seemed likely that those devices did in fact lead to a form of grammatical knowledge closer to an explicit knowledge than to the internal, self-regulating system being aimed at.[8] It also seemed likely that the most important condition for learners' abstraction of grammatical structure from relevant language samples was not so much an encounter with many samples of the same kind in quick succession but rather an intense preoccupation with the meaning of language samples – i.e. an effort to make sense of the language encountered, or to get meaning across in language adequately for given, and immediate, purposes. If this was so, the S-O-S procedure of situationalizing new language was of value not just in ensuring that the meaning of the new language was internalized along with its form but, more importantly, in bringing about in learners a preoccupation with meaning and an effort to understand. The nature of some imaginative classroom procedures being developed for communicative language teaching – such as the communicative exercise types discussed in Johnson (1982: 163–75) – also indicated an intuition about the value of a preoccupation with meaning for language learning; and Widdowson's observation that 'we do not simply measure discourse up against our knowledge of pre-existing rules; we create discourse and *commonly bring new rules into existence by so doing*' (Widdowson 1978: 69; my italics) suggested a similar perception.

Communication in the classroom – in the sense of meaning-focused activity (i.e. a process of coping with a need to make sense or get meaning across) could therefore be a good means of developing grammatical competence in learners, quite independently of the issue of developing functional or social appropriacy in language use. Further, discussion often pointed to what was clearly a fundamental question about grammatical competence, namely, its 'deployability'. True grammatical competence was seen to be deployable – in the sense that it came into play in direct response to a need to communicate – without any linguistic elicitation and with equal levels of accuracy within and outside the classroom. The observation that learners' ability to make sentences in the classroom did not carry over to other contexts indicated a lack of deployability in the form of knowledge promoted by S-O-S procedures. It seemed plausible, in contrast, that deployability would be ensured if effort to communicate was in fact the context in which knowledge of the language developed. The aim of using communication as a pedagogic procedure would thus be to develop in learners an internal system which was deployable and, when deployed, capable of achieving grammatical accuracy.

In more general terms, possible grounds for dissatisfaction with S-O-S pedagogy could be summarized as follows: those who had been taught English for several years at school were still unable:

– to use (i.e. deploy) the language when necessary outside the classroom (they found themselves deliberating unnaturally).
– to achieve an acceptable level of grammatical accuracy in their language use outside the classroom (though they might achieve such accuracy in a classroom context).
– to achieve an acceptable level of situational appropriacy in their language use outside the classroom (though they might achieve grammatical accuracy).

Although experience indicated that there was some truth to all three, the first two were seen to be much more serious and central to pedagogy than the third, and communication in the classroom (in the sense of meaning-focused activity, as indicated above) was seen to be a form of pedagogy likely to avoid those two problems. It was to indicate the difference between this particular interpretation of the nature and role of communication in pedagogy on the one hand, and forms of pedagogy which addressed themselves primarily to the third problem above on the other, that the project used the term 'communicational' teaching, instead of the more current 'communicative' teaching.

S-O-S pedagogy, too, could be said to have addressed itself to the first two problems in rejecting the teaching of explicit grammar and in seeking instead to regulate learners' internalization of the grammatical system through planned progression, pre-selection, and form-focused activity. If, however, it was meaning-focused activity which facilitated learners' subconscious abstraction of grammatical structure from the samples of language encountered in that context, then form-focused activity was a mistaken pedagogic procedure. Further, the attempt to regulate and organize samples of language in grammatical terms through planned progression and pre-selection could have been a mistake as well. The assumption behind such regulation was that the teacher, or syllabus designer, already had a description of the grammatical system which learners were to internalize and was transferring that system, part by part, to learners' subconscious minds through appropriate samples of language. But developments in grammatical theory and description, in particular transformational-generative grammar, had shown clearly that the internal grammatical system operated subconsciously by fluent speakers was vastly more complex than was reflected by, or could be incorporated into, any grammatical syllabus – so complex and inaccessible to consciousness in fact, that no grammar yet constructed by linguists was able to account for it fully.[9] Perhaps the most important implication of generative grammar for second language pedagogy was that the grammatical descriptions used for constructing syllabuses or practice materials were hopelessly inadequate as descriptions of the internal system which learners had to develop in order to achieve grammatical accuracy in their language use. It was therefore unlikely that any planned progression in a grammatical syllabus could actually reflect or regulate the development of the internal grammatical system being aimed at.

Perceptions such as these led, at the end of the second seminar, to the setting up of a teaching project with the aim of developing pedagogic procedures which would (1) bring about in the classroom a preoccupation with meaning and an effort to cope with communication and (2) avoid planned progression and pre-selection in terms of language structure as well as form-focused activity (or planned language practice) in the classroom. The main issues involved in such teaching will be examined in some detail in later chapters, which will indicate how the perceptions themselves were influenced by the experience of the project. Meanwhile, some indication of how the initial perception was actually stated at the time of setting up the project can be found in Appendix II.

Classes taught

Table 1 lists some facts about the eight classes of children taught on the project. The classes were at different schools (with the exception of numbers 7 and 8) in different towns or districts and at different stages of both schooling and instruction in English. They received project teaching for varying lengths of time (for reasons to be indicated shortly). Thus, class 1 in the table was at a secondary school in Malleswaram, initially consisted of fifty girls (see, however, below), was Standard VIII (i.e. the eighth year of a ten-year school course), was in its fourth year of instruction in English, and was taught on the project for three academic years. (An academic year is from June to the following March or April; so class 1 was taught on the project from June 1979 to March 1982.) The schools were in two different states. Classes 1, 4, and 6 were in the state of Karnataka where instruction in English begins in Standard V (age 10) and continues for six years up to the end of Standard X. Classes 2, 3, 5, 7, and 8 were in the state of Tamil Nadu where instruction in English begins in Standard III (age 8) and continues for eight years up to the end of Standard X. (For a list of all the schools see Appendix III.)

There is a public examination at the end of Standard X in each state, marking the end of secondary education. Although the syllabus in English for the successive standards is primarily a graded list of structures and vocabulary, the syllabus for the final year (Standard X) includes, in addition, a set of literary, descriptive, or discursive texts, selected without regard to the linguistic syllabus, though with some consideration of their difficulty-level in terms of both content and language. But, more importantly in relation to the project, the public examination requires students to manipulate given sentences and words (for example to rewrite sentences as directed, fill in gaps, match items in different lists, and spot or correct grammatical or lexical errors) and to reproduce the gist of the texts in the form of summaries or short essays which are often memorized in advance.[10] As a result, project teaching had either to devote some of the time in a Standard X class to summarizing texts and doing exercises on grammar and vocabulary (thus deviating from the project's principles) or to avoid teaching any class in Standard X. For this reason, only class 1 received project teaching in its Standard X year.

There is also a public examination half-way through the school course – at the end of Standard VII in Karnataka and at the end of

Table 1 Classes taught on the project

Serial number and location of class	Students	Starting stage for project teaching			Project teaching done
		On the school course	On the English course	Age	1979 1980 1981 1982 1983 1984
1 Malleswaram	50 girls	Standard VIII	4th year	13	
2 Nungambakkam	40 girls	Standard VI	4th year	11	
3 T. Nagar	30 girls + boys	Standard III	1st year	8	
4 Tasker Town	60 boys	Standard VIII	4th year	13	
5 Cuddalore	45 girls + boys	Standard III	1st year	8	
6 Jayanagar	50 girls + boys	Standard V	1st year	10	
7 Tiruvottiyur	60 boys	Standard VI	4th year	11	
8 Tiruvottiyur	55 boys	Standard VI	4th year	11	

Standard VIII in Tamil Nadu – which created greater problems for project teaching. The examination is generally modelled on that at the end of Standard X, which meant that the project had, once again, either to avoid teaching a Standard VII class (or a Standard VIII class, depending on the state) or include specific examination preparation in its teaching of such classes. More seriously, the classes in a school are almost always reorganized after a public examination, to take account of failures and students changing schools or discontinuing study, which meant that the project could not have the same group of students to teach before and after Standard VII in Karnataka and Standard VIII in Tamil Nadu. There is, in addition, a movement of students from primary to secondary (or middle) schools at the end of Standard IV in Karnataka and Standard V in Tamil Nadu, which also meant that the project could not have the same group before and after that stage. The consequence of all these institutional constraints was that no class was available for continuous teaching for more than three school years and some classes could be taught only for two years in order to avoid the year of a public examination. In two cases (classes 4 and 7), other institutional factors led to a discontinuation of teaching after only a year.

All the eight classes were in schools within the state system, where the language of instruction was the language of the state and the mother tongue of most students. They were, furthermore, schools which generally drew children from homes and social groups in which no English was spoken (and, in many instances, the mother tongue was not read or written, though the students themselves had acquired some literacy in the mother tongue at school by the time they started receiving instruction in English). They were also homes which frequently had to hold children back from attending school and sometimes to withdraw them from school altogether; so the number of children shown in the table for each class is only the initial number, which was reduced by a few students each year. There was also a high level of absenteeism (about 15 per cent of the class, on average) all the time.

The time given to English in the schools is one teaching period of forty minutes a day, five days a week in some schools and six in others. A year's teaching of English amounts to about 130 teaching periods, which works out at about ninety contact hours (not counting the absenteeism mentioned above which reduces this time for particular students). Project teaching of a given class meant that all teaching of English for that class was done according to the project's principles, thus ignoring the syllabus and course-books laid down by the state system. No change was made in other aspects of the teaching situation such as class composition, timetabling or physical facilities. Some of the classes involved in the project were at a post-initial stage (i.e. fourth year) of learning English while others were beginners. There was one post-initial class in the first year of the project and two in the second. In the third year, there were three post-initial classes and one class of beginners. In the fourth and fifth years, there were three beginners' classes and one post-initial class. In general, most of the work was done with post-initial classes in the earlier stages of the project, while in the later stages the emphasis shifted to beginners.[11]

Teachers

Those who did the teaching on the project were either specialists (i.e. teacher trainers or teachers with specialist qualifications in teaching English) or regular teachers at schools. The first two project classes were taught entirely by specialists, while the teaching of the third class was shared between a specialist and a teacher at the school concerned. The fourth class was taught by specialists, while the fifth and sixth classes were taught partly by specialists and partly by regular teachers. The seventh and eight classes were taught entirely by regular teachers. Teaching can thus be seen to have passed, in a limited way, from specialists to regular teachers.

Eighteen people in all participated in the teaching, nine of them teacher trainers by profession, two university teachers, three members of the British Council's specialist staff in India, and four regular teachers in the schools concerned. They are referred to as the 'project team' (or 'project group') in this book but did not in fact function as a single team at any stage. The fourteen specialists were all in full-time employment in various institutions and were taking up project teaching as a voluntary part-time activity for the length of time (one, two, or three years) that was convenient for them. Those who functioned as a team in any one year were those who were doing the teaching in that year – four to eight teachers. There was also a geographical separation of up to 200 miles between different project classes and schools, which meant that only those who were teaching the same class (two or three teachers) were in daily contact with each other.

Principles and procedures

Teaching in the first year

Project teaching in much of the first year was marked by uncertainty about procedures, repeated disappointments, conflicting perceptions or interpretations of particular lessons, and a good deal of negative response from learners. The project group (consisting of four teachers at that time) had a general concept of what it wished to bring about in the classroom, namely a preoccupation in learners with meaning and a resultant effort to understand and say things; it also had a clear notion of the procedures it wished to avoid, namely pre-selection of language and form-focused activity. It had, however, few ideas about what procedures it could or wished to follow. Among those which seemed to be promising at the time were story completion – the teacher telling a story up to the point considered most interesting and then inviting students to suggest possible conclusions, simulation (involving role-play or dramatization), puzzles of various kinds, and 'real-life talk' – the teacher and learners talking to one another, as they would outside the classroom, about themselves, their views, or their experiences. Story completion was attempted repeatedly, but generally failed to evoke the response expected. If the class did not find the story particularly interesting, there was little desire to try to complete it; and if the story did prove to be interesting, there was a demand that the teacher go on to tell the rest of it, and a sense of resentment when this was not done. Simulation quickly showed itself to be unsuitable: it was difficult to find situations which were associated with the use of English in India and accessible to the students' experience; and the students, in any case, regarded such activity as non-serious and would only engage in it as deliberate language practice work (that is, with the sentences they were to say provided to them in advance). Puzzles turned out to be too demanding (for example difficult to state in simple language without destroying their cognitive challenge) and also too unrelatable to one another to support any sustained and structured activity. Real-life talk conflicted directly with notions about the classroom and was persistently viewed by learners as only a friendly preliminary to more serious work rather than as a serious activity in itself.

In more general terms, there was a lack of shared expectations between teachers and learners which could enable each to interpret and evaluate the actions of the other. There was also a lack of stable patterning to different lessons such that it would indicate criteria of relevance and make it possible to accomodate unpredicted responses. The learners were facing not only new forms of classroom activity but new concepts of what classroom activity should be about; and the teacher's own sense of uncertainty about classroom procedures was not reassuring to them. For their part, the teachers were facing not only dissatisfaction with particular lessons but also difficulty in identifying the sources of dissatisfaction. As a result, they had problems in adjusting teaching during the course of a lesson so as to avoid or reduce felt dissatisfaction, and generally in using the experience of each lesson to ensure greater satisfaction in the next.[12]

Task and pre-task

Gradually, however, the problems began to clarify themselves and criteria for assessing particular lessons began to emerge. It was noticed that whenever there was a piece of logical thinking in-volved in a teacher-class exchange it was possible for the teacher to meet wrong responses (or non-response) from the class by breaking down the logical process into smaller steps, such that the class saw a general direction (and destination) to the sequence of steps and in the meantime found each step easy enough to take. The result was a sequence of exchanges with a perceived purpose and a clear outcome which was satisfying both to the teacher because it was a structured activity, and to learners because there was a clear criterion of success and a sense of achievement from success. Such a sequence gave the teacher ongoing and relatively unambiguous evidence of learners' involvement in the process and opportunities to adjust his or her own part in the interchange in the light of that evidence: the relevance and readiness of learners' responses indicated how far they were keeping pace with the logical steps being taken, and it was relatively easy for the teacher to make the next step smaller or larger accordingly. Teacher-class negotiation – in the sense of a sequence of exchanges connecting one point to another on a given line of thought and adjustable at any point as it occurs – was thus identified as a classroom procedure which was both feasible and desirable. Opportunity for such negotiation became an important consideration in selecting classroom activities, and it was recognized that negotiation was most likely to take place – and to prove satisfying – when the demand on thinking made by the activity was just above the level which learners could meet without help. An activity which required learners to arrive at an outcome from given information through some process of thought, and which allowed teachers to control and regulate that process, was regarded as a 'task'.

A related observation was that the learners' perception of the piece of thinking they had to do in any given instance was based largely on what parallel they saw between that instance and another, and that such analogic thought was a useful resource for the teacher both in getting learners to understand the task being set and in guiding their effort to carry it out. This meant that the piece of logical thinking demanded by a given task could be made clear not only by attempting to explain the logic involved but, much more easily and usefully, by setting a parallel task which was either simpler or more accessible to learners in some way, or which was worked out by the teacher himself or by some specially able students in the class, thus providing the necessary help. Such parallelism also meant that some students could learn to do what was demanded of them by observing others meeting a similar demand, and the class as such could attempt to do a task without the teacher's guidance after the experience of doing a similar task with the teacher's help.

Observations such as these led in due course to a clear preference for classroom activities which involved learners in some form of reasoning, or inferring, or inter-relating information in a logical way. They also led to a recurrent pattern to each lesson. There were now at least two parallel tasks in each lesson. The first, called perhaps misleadingly 'pre-task', was to be attempted as a whole-class activity, under the teacher's guidance and control.[13] The second, called 'task' in contrast to the pre-task, was to be attempted by each learner individually (or sometimes in voluntary collaboration with a fellow-learner) with assistance sought from the teacher when necessary on specific points. There was also a third component to each lesson, consisting of a quick marking of students' individual work (i.e. the outcome of the 'task' stated by each student on paper). This marking was done, usually overnight, on the basis of content, not language, and was meant both to give students some feedback on their level of success and, equally, to give the teacher some idea of the level of challenge the task had presented.[14] The teacher's assessment of the level of difficulty acted as an input to the planning of subsequent lessons.

The basic format of the whole-class activity was teacher-class interaction in the form of question and answer (or instruction and compliance) which served three functions: (1) it led the class, step by step, to the expected outcome of the pre-task, thus involving exchanges each of which called for a greater effort of reasoning than the last; (2) it broke down a given step further into smaller steps when a need for doing so was indicated by learners' responses, and (3) it provided one or more parallels to one or more of the steps in reasoning, ensuring that as many students as possible in a mixed-ability class grasped the nature of the activity. The proportion between these three functions varied from one lesson and one class to another depending on the ease or difficulty with which the class was, in the teacher's judgement, able to make the effort called for. The teacher's plan for the pre-task normally consisted, in addition to whatever factual information the pre-task was based on, of a set of graded questions or instructions serving the first function, and one or more parallel questions/instructions to be used when necessary, serving the third. Questions/instructions to serve any further negotiation (i.e. the second function above, of breaking down a step into still smaller steps) were thought up in the classroom when the teacher felt they were needed. The parallel questions were used or omitted, or added to in the light of perceived need, and the teacher sometimes omitted some of the graded questions as well – either the last ones, if the class found the pre-task more difficult than anticipated (and therefore needed many more questions of the other two kinds), or the earlier, easier ones if the planned grading was found to be needlessly detailed. The teacher's plan also, of course, included a task similar to the pre-task, though never identical and not of a kind which could be performed without fresh, though similar, thinking, along with a set of similarly graded questions.

These principles for structuring a single lesson were then used to structure a sequence of lessons: tasks of the same type – that is, based on the same body of information or the same format – were set on successive days such that each day's work was similar to but more complex than the previous day's. Further, when the teacher felt that all, or most, of the class needed to attempt more work at the same level before they could attempt anything more complex, a whole lesson was made parallel to the previous day's, in the same way that pre-task and task were parallel to each other or certain questions within the pre-task were parallel to others. Parallel lessons were especially useful in alternating between oral and written media: parallel pre-tasks and tasks (i.e. the factual information involved and/or a set of questions/instructions) were regularly presented to learners in writing after similar pre-tasks or tasks had been attempted by them from an oral presentation. The project team found that, judging from learners' performance, the change to the written medium in itself constituted an increase in complexity. This ordering of oral and written tasks is the only piece of deliberate *linguistic* grading which was used in project teaching. The other traditional form of grading – reception followed by production – was viewed quite differently and will be discussed in Chapter 4.

Language control

As project teaching became more and more structured along these lines, it was also realized that this structuring brought about a form of simplification and control of the teacher's language in the classroom which was different in quality from planned language control, but entirely adequate to sustain classroom interaction. In the early stages of project teaching, teachers had found themselves uncertain about the extent to which they had to simplify their language, and dissatisfied with having to check at regular intervals on learners' comprehension with questions such as 'Do you understand?' or 'What did I say?'[15] With the emergence of task-based interaction, in which each step was a teacher-class exchange that influenced the next, there was now a clear criterion of adequacy for simplification, namely that the class should be able to grasp the current step in the task, as well as constant feedback from learners. When there was an indication of incomprehension, the teacher adopted such strategies as repeating or rephrasing the statement, breaking it down into smaller propositions, employing a non-verbal form of communication, or providing a gloss in the learners' mother-tongue, for the purpose of getting the meaning across adequately for the class to make a relevant response. It was also observed that task-based interaction was itself a context which facilitated comprehension since there were only limited possibilities, in any given exchange, of what something could mean. Comprehension and inferencing were further facilitated by the parallel patterns of discourse resulting from similar or contrasting pieces of reasoning at different points in the task. Indeed, it was a pleasant surprise for the project group to realize how far task-based interaction ensured adequate simplification and comprehension without any prior linguistic planning. It was not of course assumed that all the language used in the classroom was being fully comprehended by learners, but, as will be argued in Chapter 3, 'full comprehension' is not a usable concept in any case.

Meaning-focused activity

Experience of task-based teaching also helped to clarify the project group's notions about learners' preoccupation with language and meaning. This can perhaps be stated in terms of four categories of classroom activity:

1 *Rule-focused activity* in which learners are occupied with a conscious perception or application (or memorization or recall) of the rules of language structure. This kind of activity involves understanding how the language concerned 'works' and was rejected by S-O-S pedagogy, as noted earlier, on the grounds that such explicit knowledge of the rules did not lead to an ability to use the language automatically.

2 *Form-focused activity* in which learners are occupied with repeating or manipulating given language forms, or constructing new forms on the model of those given. Such 'practice' activity is valued by S-O-S pedagogy on the grounds that it facilitates subconscious assimilation of the structural regularities inherent in the forms involved and promotes automaticity in language use. It also relates to the notion of language 'skills', both in the sense of automaticity in use and in the sense of providing experience in the different modes of listening, speaking, reading, and writing.

3 *Meaningful activity* in which learners repeat, manipulate, or construct language forms with attention not only to the forms themselves but to the meanings or contexts which are associated with them. Such 'meaningful practice' is also valued by S-O-S pedagogy on the grounds that it ensures the assimilation both of structural regularities and of their associated meanings or contexts.

4 *Meaning-focused activity* in which learners are occupied with understanding, extending (e.g. through reasoning), or conveying meaning, and cope with language forms as demanded by that process. Attention to language forms is thus not intentional but incidental to perceiving, expressing, and organizing meaning.

There are, no doubt, forms of activity which fall between any two of these categories, but this categorization indicates how the project group saw the difference in classroom activity-types between S-O-S pedagogy and project teaching. Project teaching aimed at meaning-focused activity to the exclusion of the other three types. Task-based interaction in the classroom constituted meaning-focused activity in that not only was the interaction directed, at each point and as a whole, to outcomes in terms of meaning-content but the meaning-content involved at any point was determined by ongoing exchanges and had to be responsive to unpredicted contributions. Language use in such a process could only be contingent upon meaning-exchange and any attention to language forms as such was necessarily incidental to communication.

The format of task-based teaching conformed reasonably well to both learners' and teachers' notions of classroom activity. The pre-task stage of the lesson, normally occupying between a half and two-thirds of the time, was given to teacher-directed, whole-class activity while the rest was used by learners for working on their own on an 'assignment' related to what had gone before. What was being dealt with in both parts was meaning-content requiring mental effort. The whole-class activity consisted of a pedagogic dialogue in which the teacher's questions were, as in other classrooms, invitations to learners to demonstrate their ability, not pretended requests for enlightenment, and learner's responses arose from their role as learners, not from assumed roles in simulated situations or from their individual lives outside the classroom.

Teaching in subsequent years

The ideas outlined above took shape towards the end of the first year of project teaching. They were implemented in the second year's teaching of the same class (Class 1 in Table 1) and, more consistently, in the teaching of a new class (Class 2 in Table 1) which was added to the project at that point. This new class was taught for two years (275 lessons in all) and the tasks devised in the course of that teaching formed a repertoire for use with later post-initial classes. Meanwhile, two further classes were added to the project at the beginning of the third year, one of which (Class 3 in Table 1) was of beginners. The project group felt that it had by then gained sufficient understanding of task-based teaching (and sufficient classroom confirmation of its perceptions) for an attempt to be made to extend teaching to beginner level.

Contrary to the group's fears, task-based teaching of beginners did not throw up any major problems requiring a re-thinking of the principles. One small advantage was the existence of several

English loan-words in everyday use in Indian languages, and in the school 'dialects', some of which were therefore available even in the first lesson for beginners. Examples are 'blackboard', 'chalk', 'notebook', 'first', 'last', 'map', 'drawing', 'timetable', and 'bell'. Basic literacy in English was a specific aim at beginner level, and was achieved by using letters of the alphabet regularly as 'coins of the game' in various tasks – for naming parts of given drawings, for instance, or labelling locations or placement in given configurations. (An example will be given later in this chapter.) Early tasks also drew a good deal on learners' numeracy, using forms of information normally expressed in numbers such as times of day, dates on calendars, age and year of birth, prices, and numbers of objects bought, lost, or saved. The cognitive challenge of such tasks generally consisted of counting and calculating. The verbal negotiation which took place in these contexts (and which required surprisingly little mother-tongue glossing – only about two words in a lesson) increased learners' familiarity with English, which made it possible to base subsequent tasks on verbally-expressed information.

In general, teaching beginners made two things forcefully clear. First, tasks in the classroom create a need to communicate which brings into play not just target-language resources, but all the other resources learners have at their disposal, for example conjecture, gestures, knowledge of conventions, numeracy, and the mother tongue. When target-language resources are unavailable the others are used to extra effect to compensate for that lack. It is therefore not the case that beginners in a given language are unable to engage in any communication in that language: when focused on communication, they are able to deploy non-linguistic resources and, as a result, not only achieve some degree of communication but, in the process, some new resources, however small, in the target language. These, in turn, are deployed in the next attempt at communication, yielding further target-language resources. Such acquisition of target-language resources and their deployment to maximal effect reveals itself dramatically in early lessons with beginners. Secondly, tasks in the classroom, and the interaction which they produce, are a powerful support to the learner's effort to infer meaning, and consequently to the acquisition of target-language resources, since they set up explicit frames of reference, rules of relevance, recurrent procedures and reasoning patterns, parallel situations, and problem-and-solution sequences, all of which facilitate comprehension, as noted earlier, and reduce the insecurity of action based on random conjecture.

The tasks devised in the course of a year's teaching of beginners (Class 3 in Table 1) formed a repertoire to draw on in teaching two other classes of beginners (Classes 5 and 6), which started at the beginning of the fourth year of the project. All three classes of beginners were able, after a year's project teaching, to cope with tasks which had been devised earlier for post-initial (fourth-year English) classes, so that there was now a collection of tasks for about 400 lessons from the beginning stage. While a part of this collection (tasks devised for Class 3 in its first year) was, as just noted, re-used later by other teachers with two other classes, the rest (tasks devised for Class 2 in the two years that class was taught) was re-used by other teachers with three subsequent project classes (Classes 4, 7, and 8). This indicates the amount of actual replication which the project was able to achieve.

Review seminars

A review seminar, of one to two weeks, was organized at the end of each year's project teaching with roughly the same types of audience as at the two seminars which led to the project.[16] Not only were lesson reports on the year's teaching (as illustrated in the next section) made available at these seminars, but some actual samples of teaching – in the form of audio-recordings, transcripts, live lessons with one of the project classes and, to a very limited extent, video-recordings – were provided for examination and comment. The project team's interpretation of the teaching was also presented and discussed from different points of view, as were the views of those outside the project team who had taken the trouble during the year to observe some part of project teaching.

Reactions to the project were varied and often in conflict with one another, but the seminar discussions caused at least a re-examination of past pedagogic assumptions and often a sharing, corroboration, or modification of different perceptions.

Evaluation

One result of the discussion at review seminars was a decision by the project team to arrange for an external evaluation of learners' progress. Four different project classes (Classes 3, 5, 6, and 8 in Table 1) were given a series of tests, along with their non-project peers in the schools concerned, at the end of the fifth year. A brief report on this evaluation can be found in Beretta and Davies (1984) which is reprinted as Appendix VI.

Illustrative tasks

Some examples of the types of task used in project teaching are given below. They are taken from the brief lesson-reports which were made available for comment and criticism in the first three years of the project to all who were interested, including those who attended annual review seminars. It must be remembered in reading these examples that such task specification does not constitute language-teaching material in the usual sense: it represents only an indication of content, leaving the actual language to be negotiated in each classroom; and even the content is subject to modification for particular classes and in particular lessons. A comparison between the 'Railway timetables' lesson report given immediately below and the transcript of the same lesson which appears in Appendix IVa will illustrate this negotiability of tasks.[17]

1 Railway timetables

This was the first task, in a sequence of five, based on railway timetables. The teacher knew that students in the class were not familiar with railway timetables, though all of them had seen trains and more than half of them had been in a train at some time. The teacher also knew that the class was quite unfamiliar with the twenty-four hour clock and therefore did a preliminary pre-task (relying on parallels to give students the concept) and task, before going on to work based on a timetable as such.

Preliminary pre-task The teacher writes '0600 hours = 6 am' on the blackboard and gets students to suggest similar twelve-hour clock equivalents of such times as 0630, 0915, 1000, 1145, 1200, 1300, 2300, 0000, 0115, and 0430. Pupils do this with reasonable success, although counting sometimes proves difficult (for example 2015 minus 1200), and the meaning of 0000 hours proves quite beyond them.

Preliminary task The teacher writes up eight twenty-four hour clock timings on the blackboard and students individually work out and write in their notebooks the twelve-hour equivalent of each. The teacher then writes up the answers and students mark each other's work. The result, from a show of hands, indicates that almost exactly half the students got five or more answers right and the rest four or less.

Pre-task The following is written up on the blackboard:

	Madras	**Katpadi**	**Jolarpet**	**Bangalore**
Brindavan	Dep. 0725	Arr. 0915	Arr. 1028	Arr. 1300
Express		Dep. 0920	Dep. 1030	

Questions such as the following are asked, answered, and discussed:

1 When does the Brindavan Express leave Madras/arrive in Bangalore? (Answers are expected in terms of the twelve-hour clock.)
2 When does it arrive at Katpadi/leave Jolarpet?
3 For how long does it stop at Jolarpet?
4 How long does it take to go from Madras to Katpadi/ Jolarpet to Bangalore?
5 How many stations does it stop at on the way?

Task Sheets of paper containing the following timetable and the questions below it are handed out. The teacher asks a few questions orally, based on an anticipation of learners' difficulties (for example, 'Is this a day train or a night train?' in view of the difference from the pre-task timetable, and 'For how long does the train stop at Jolarpet?' in view of students' observed difficulty in calculating time across the hour mark) and then leaves the class to do the task.

	Madras	**Arkonam**	**Katpadi**	**Jolarpet**	**Kolar**	**Bangalore**
Bangalore	Dep. 2140	Arr. 2250	Arr. 0005	Arr. 0155	Arr. 0340	Arr. 0550
Mail		Dep. 2305	Dep. 0015	Dep. 0210	Dep. 0350	

1 When does the Bangalore Mail leave Madras?
2 When does it arrive in Bangalore?
3 For how long does it stop at Arkonam?
4 At what time does it reach Katpadi?
5 At what time does it leave Jolarpet?
6 How long does it take to go from Madras to Arkonam?
7 How long does it take to go from Kolar to Bangalore?

Students' performance:

7 or 6 answers correct	14 students
5 or 4 answers correct	8 students
3 or 2 answers correct	6 students
1 or 0 answers correct	3 students

The next lesson based on railway timetables presented students with the following task (following a similar pre-task) as representing an appropriate increase in complexity:

	Madras	Arkonam	Katpadi	Jolarpet	Kolar	Bangalore
Bangalore Mail	Dep. 2140	Arr. 2255 Dep. 2305	Arr. 0005 Dep. 0015	Arr. 0155 Dep. 0210	Arr. 0340 Dep. 0350	Arr. 0550
Bangalore Express	Dep. 1300	Arr. 1420 Dep. 1440	Arr. 1515 Dep. 1520	Arr. 1647 Dep. 1650	Arr. 1825 Dep. 1830	Arr. 2020
Brindavan Express	Dep. 0725	—	Arr. 0915 Dep. 0920	Arr. 1028 Dep. 1030	—	Arr. 1300

Questions:

1 When does the Bangalore Express arrive at Katpadi?
2 At what time does the Bangalore Mail leave Arkonam?
3 For how long does the Bangalore Express stop at Jolarpet?
4 Which trains stop at Arkonam?
5 Where is the Brindavan Express at twelve noon?
6 Where is the Bangalore Express at three p.m.?
7 Mr Ganeshan wants to travel from Madras to Kolar. He has some work in Kolar in the morning. By which train should he travel?
8 Mrs Mani has to work in Madras on the morning of Monday. She wants to get to Bangalore on Monday night. Which train can she take?

A later task in the sequence involved filling in request forms (used in India) for railway reservations. The form requires such details as the number of the train, date of travel, the traveller's age, class of travel, and form of accommodation (seat/berths), which were made available to the class in the form of personal letters received from friends or relatives – living elsewhere – asking for reservations to be made for their intended travel.

2 Instructions to draw

A sequence of lessons based on instructions to draw contained the following task (following a similar pre-task) representing an appropriate challenge at one stage of project teaching:

a Draw a line, from left to right.
b Write B at the right end of the line, and A at the left end.
c Draw another line below AB.
d Write D at its left end and C at its right end.
e Join BD.

When the sequence was resumed two weeks later, with twelve lessons on other task-types intervening, the following task proved to be appropriately challenging for the class. (The pre-task which preceded it introduced conventions such as that 'continue AB' meant continuing the line concerned in the direction of B to about twice its original length.)

a Name the top corners of the square: B on the left and C on the right.
b Name the corners at the bottom: D on the right and A on the left.
c Continue AB and call the end of the line E.
d Continue CD and write F at the end of the line.
e Join EC.
f What should be joined next?

Returning to the drawing sequence a long time later (when about 200 lessons had intervened, though only three of them had been on drawing instructions) the teacher found the class able to do the following task with about the same measure of success:

a Draw two parallel, horizontal lines. Let them be about four inches long.
b Join the ends of the two lines on the left, with a short vertical line.
c Use two parallel, vertical lines to join the right ends of the horizontal lines.
d Mark the mid-points of the parallel, vertical lines.
e Draw a dotted line, horizontally, passing through the mid-points of the parallel vertical lines and extending to the right for about half an inch.
f Use straight lines to join the right end of the dotted line with the right ends of the two horizontal parallel lines.

3 Interpreting rules

In a sequence of tasks based on rules of various kinds, the following was a lesson based on local rules for concessional bus fares for students. The rules (which students were given copies of) are stated first, followed by the questions which constituted the pre-task and task.

Pallavan Transport Corporation
(Madras City)

a Students can buy and use bus tokens for a month, instead of buying a ticket for each bus journey.

b The cost of tokens is as follows:

30 tokens	Rs 7.50
60 tokens	Rs 15.00
90 tokens	Rs 22.50
120 tokens	Rs 30.00

c A student has to buy at least 30 tokens a month. He/she cannot buy more than 120 tokens a month.

d One token is equal to one bus ticket: the student has to give a token to the conductor of the bus, instead of buying a ticket from him.

e Tokens should be used only for the purpose of travelling between one's home and the school or college where one is studying.

f Tokens should be bought each month between the 1st and the 15th. They can be used only between the 16th of that month and the 15th of the next month.

g No money will be refunded on unused tokens.

h Only full-time students of a school, college, or university can buy and use bus tokens. They have to produce a certificate from the head of the institution to show that they are full-time students.

i Tokens cannot be transferred from one person to another.

j If a student misuses his/her tokens, he/she will not be allowed to buy any more tokens during that year.

Pre-task After a glossing, at the students' request, of some words (for example 'refunded', 'misused') and a preliminary discussion, involving questions, about the nature of some rules (for example on the point that tokens can be bought only in multiples of thirty and that a direct bus from home to school involves the use of a single token while a change of buses involves using one token on each bus), the following case is discussed as the pre-task:

Raman is a student of the Government Arts College in Nandanam. He lives in T. Nagar. He has classes from Monday to Friday each week and eats his lunch at the college canteen. There are direct buses from T. Nagar to Nandanam.

1 How many bus tokens does Raman need each week?
2 How many tokens does he need for a month (i.e. 4 weeks, by convention)?
3 A bus ticket from T. Nagar to Nandanam costs Rs 0.50. How much does Raman save by buying tokens?
4 How many tokens should he buy each month? Why? How many will he actually use?
5 Raman's brother goes to a High School in Saidapet. Can he use Raman's extra tokens? How do you know?
6 Raman goes to see his uncle in K. K. Nagar every Sunday. Can he use his tokens to go to K. K. Nagar? How do you know?

Task Balan studies at the Higher Secondary School in Nungambakkam. His home is in Adyar. He has classes only in the afternoons, from Monday to Saturday. There are direct buses from Nungambakkam to Adyar and a ticket costs one rupee.

1 How many tokens does Balan need each month?
2 How many tokens should he buy each month? How much money does he save?
3 He bought 60 tokens in July. His school had some holidays in August, so he used only 30 tokens up to 15 August.
  a Can he go on using the remaining 30 tokens? How do you know?
  b Can he return the remaining 30 tokens and get back the money? How can you tell?

One of the students, who belonged to the top half of the class in terms of general performance, wrote the following answer:

1 Balan needs every month 52 tokens (4 days holidays).

2
Balan buys 52 tickets	Rs 52.00
He buys 60 tokens	Rs 15.00
He saves	Rs 37.00

3 a He cannot use them, see Rule No. 6 of P.T.C.
  b He cannot return tickets and cannot get money, see Rule 7.

Another student, representing the lower half of the ability range in the class, wrote:

1 Balan every month need 48 tokens.
2 Balan save if he buys 60 tokens 28.00.
3 a 1st and 15th. They can used 16th and 15th of next month.
  b Only 30 tokens buy a month.

The class did four more lessons based on the same rules, two of them involving students who had to change buses between home and school (and could make an additional saving by using tokens only on the longer sector, for some days in a month); another involving irregular uses of tokens and the consequences, and yet another involving procedures for buying tokens (e.g. producing certificates, making applications). There were also sequences of tasks based on the rules for a bank account, a system of postal code numbers (and a quick mail service) used in India, and the rules of a library.

4 Beginners' tasks

Some of the tasks for beginners deliberately used the letters of the alphabet in order to lead towards literacy, as noted earlier (see page 29). The following are two examples of such tasks, with an indication of the pre-task discourse which resulted:

a On the blackboard:

Teacher talk:

I want someone to write 'b' at the end of line number five. Who can write 'b' at the end of five? Can you? . . . Come and try. Is that line five? No, that's line number one. This is line five. All right, write 'b' at the end of it . . . at the end, not in the middle. . . . No, not at the beginning, at the end. . . . Yes, write 'b' there. Good, you can go back now. . . . Now, I want someone else to write 'e' at the top of line eight. Can you? . . . Can you? Who else can? All right, you try . . . top of eight, correct. What should you write there? Not 'c', that is 'c'. I want 'e'. Yes, that's 'e', fine. Well done. Next, you have to write 'a' at the beginning of twelve.

Those who can, put up your hands. Any more? All right, you can come and write. Where is the beginning of twelve? Where is twelve? Can you find twelve there? No? Who wants to show twelve to him? Come along. That is right, number twelve. That is line twelve. Now you have to write 'a' at the beginning of that line . . . 'a' at the beginning . . . Good. . . .

b On the blackboard:

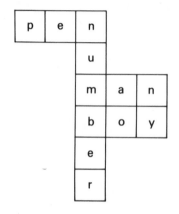

Teacher talk:

Listen to this and say whether it is true or false . . . 'a' is to the right of 'm' . . . 'a' to the right of 'm'. Is that true or false? Hands up those who say it is true. . . . What do you think? False? Let's see. Where is 'a'? And where is 'm'? . . . 'm' not 'n'. That's right, 'm'. Now, is 'a' to the right or left? To the right, correct. 'a' is to the right of 'm'. So it is true. . . . Can you see? All right. And now, listen again. Is this true or false? . . . 'u' is just above 'n' . . . just above 'n', not below. True or false? False? How can you tell? Which is 'n' and which is 'u'? Which is below? . . . 'n' is below 'u'? Above, yes. Is 'u' below or above 'n'? Below, yes. So 'u' is below 'n', not above. The statement is false. Good. . . .

It turned out that students in the beginners' class did not yet know how to read time from the clock and a sequence of lessons was accordingly based on that subject. Early tasks in the sequence involved telling time from clock faces (drawn on the blackboard) with the hands on the hour mark and half-hour mark, while later tasks involved moving one of the clock's hands according to the movement of the other, or re-positioning both hands according to specified lapses of time. This was followed by another sequence of graded tasks which involved the daily routines, for example office hours, of individuals and working out from them either the duration of particular activities, for example travel from hospital to home in the case of a doctor, or the locations of particular individuals at given times. A further sequence was based on a given monthly calendar: an early task involved relating specified dates to days of the week and vice versa, while later tasks involved relating weekly or fortnightly routines to the relevant dates, monthly routines to relevant days of the week in a given month, and working back or forward to a relevant date or day of the week in the preceding or following month.

School timetables themselves formed the basis of yet another sequence of tasks. An early task in the sequence involved filling up a blank timetable from the teacher's statements (see Appendix IVb for a transcript of the resulting pre-task discourse on one occasion) while later tasks involved relating the timetables of different classes, for example to find out when a student in one class could pass on a shared atlas or box of mathematical instruments to another in another class, or constructing from class timetables the individual timetable for a given teacher who teaches particular subjects to particular classes. A more advanced task was to find out when the head teacher could see three different teachers together during school time without disturbing any of the classes, which involved working out a time when none of the three teachers was teaching any class.

Task sequencing

As will have been gathered from the above, tasks within a given sequence (i.e. tasks of the same type forming the basis of several lessons) were ordered by a commonsense judgement of increasing complexity, the later tasks being either inclusive of the earlier ones or involving a larger amount of information, or an extension of the kind of reasoning done earlier. The following is one example:

a Given the map of a town (with the roads and some places named) marking on it or naming some other places (e.g. a hospital) on the basis of given descriptions, or describing the locations of some places in relation to others. This involves, among other things, a directional orientation on the map (e.g. 'A' is just to the north of 'B', 'C' is at the eastern end of the road, etc.)

b On the same map, stating the best (e.g. shortest, easiest) way from one place to another.

c Given someone who has lost his/her way and is now at a certain place on the same map, deciding where he/she must have gone wrong and what is best done now.

d Given bus-routes and taxi-stands on the same map, deciding which among possible routes is likely to be the best (e.g. quickest, cheapest, or with the least distance to walk) for a particular person in a particular context.

e Given the same map, deciding on the most needed new bus-route or taxi-stand (from considerations such as the locations of the railway station, the temple, the school, etc.).

There was usually more than one lesson at each level of complexity, with some variation from one to the next and with a transition from orally-presented tasks to those presented on paper, as indicated earlier. Any sequence planned or taken over from earlier teaching of another class was subject to change in the light of learners' performance in each lesson. The order in which different task sequences followed each other was similarly a matter of common-sense judgement and past experience, subject to some alterations at each re-use. A classified, and highly generalized, list of the types of task used on the project is given in Appendix V.[18]

Notes

1 Some documentation of these changes can be found in the Nagpur Report (1958), Study Group Report (1967), and Study Group Report (1971).

2 See Smith (1962) and Smith (1968: 180–205) for a description of the programme, and Widdowson (1968: 115–17) for some comment.

3 The RIE Bulletins published in 1978 and 1979 provide summaries of the proceedings of these two seminars.

4 See Palmer (1921: 54–5): 'Proficiency in the understanding of the structure of a language is attained by treating the subject as a science, by studying the *theory*; but proficiency in the *use* of a language can only come as a result of perfectly formed habit. . . . If we are unaware of the manner in which we have pieced [a sentence] together, we have produced it automatically. . . . If we build it up by conscious synthesis or by a rapid translation from an equivalent sentence of our native tongue, we do not produce it automatically; we have not formed the

habit of using the sentence or the type of sentence to which it belongs.'

5 Some examples are Allen and Widdowson (1974), Morrow and Johnson (1979), Johnson and Morrow (1979).

6 See van Ek (1975, 1980).

7 See Wilkins (1976). Also Wilkins (1981: 99): 'In the worldwide reality of language teaching, a notional syllabus may force the teacher's attention on meaning where, even if contrary to intention, with a structural syllabus meaning is often neglected.'

8 The distinction being made here between explicit and implicit knowledge is close to that made by Bialystok (1978; 1983) except that Bialystok regards implicit knowledge as being 'unanalysed' (1983: 106) and the process of inferencing in language acquisition as leading only to explicit knowledge (1978: 79; 1983: 105). I regard implicit knowledge as being an analysed (hence generative) system and subconscious inferencing as a process which helps to develop it.

9 cf. Chomsky (1976: 4): 'For the conscious mind, not specifically designed for the purpose, it remains a distant goal to reconstruct and comprehend what the child has done intuitively and with minimal effort.' Also Chomsky (1980: 133): 'Ordinary grammar books, quite properly for their purposes, tacitly assume a principled grammar (generally without awareness) and deal with idiosyncrasies, with the kinds of things which could not be known without experience or instruction. . . . Explanatory principles with any merit bearing on the domain of facts of the sort I have been considering are in general inaccessible to consciousness, and there is no reason to expect otherwise.' Palmer had pointed out, too, that the system that is learnt in learning a second language 'is so complex and so vast that the learned world has not yet succeeded in unravelling it or in sounding its depths' (1921: 2).

10 This shows the problem in acting on Brumfit's suggestion that since the public examination is 'a test designed to measure structural competence in English' and since the project's 'hypothesis is that a problem-solving approach is effective in teaching the structure of the language, such a public examination should have some validity' as an evaluation of the project (1984b: 238).

11 Hence Brumfit's remark, based on the project's situation in 1982, that 'most of the students taught have not been beginners' (1984a: 238). The project team stated its reasons for starting with a post-initial class as follows (RIE Newsletter 1/1, July 1979): 'There are two major assumptions in a communicational approach to school-level teaching, viz. (a) that language "use" (in Widdowson's sense) is not merely a matter of exploiting the language structure already learnt for communicative purposes, but constitutes a good pedagogic device for enlarging the learner's command of language structure itself, and (b) that all language structure can, in principle, be taught and learnt through activities involving language use. We think that the second assumption is not only bolder than the first but is based on the validity of it. The first assumption can be true without the second being true but not vice versa. Testing the first assumption, therefore, seems to us both a simpler task (with independent potential for useful findings) and a necessary step towards testing the second.'

12 Reviewing the teaching done in the first three months, the project team said (RIE Newsletter 1/2, September 1979): 'In the process of ignoring the specific principles of structural teaching, we run the risk (and have already been guilty to some extent) of ignoring the more general principles of all teaching, such as (i) pitching (and adjusting in the light of experience) the level of activity or effort to the actual ability of learners, (ii) grading a sequence of activities from simple to more complex, so as to produce a cumulative effect, (iii) the need for teacher–learner rapport based, for example, on continuity between lessons and the building up of appropriate learner-expectations, and (iv) the need for (and modes of) reward/reinforcement, feedback and economy.'

Assessing the teaching done in the course of the first year, the project team regarded 56 of the 126 lessons taught as unsuccessful and the remaining 70 as successful, according to the following criteria: 'A lesson has been considered successful if (i) it had a task-centred pattern, and (ii) the task set seemed to engage most pupils' minds, i.e. the task was perceived clearly and attempted seriously, regardless of what measure of success was actually achieved. Unsuccessful lessons are those which (i) were not task-centred, i.e. were devoted entirely to preparation/practice or set the task too late for it be attempted, or (ii) were too difficult, hence brought forth random responses, or (iii) were too easy as a result of over-guidance, thus reducing the task almost to mere reproduction, or (iv) proved, for some reason, uninteresting (or "silly") to pupils or (v) very occasionally, were frustrated by external factors, e.g. last day of term; a school event.' (RIE Newsletter 1/4, April 1980).

13 The term 'pre-task' has been mistakenly understood as involving direct teaching (i.e. presentation and practice) of the concepts as well as the items of language needed for the task: connections tend to be established in the minds of those who read reports on project teaching between 'pre-task', 'pre-teaching', 'preparation', and 'presentation'. Johnson's (1982: 141) interpretation of the pre-task in these terms may, in addition, have arisen from the fact that he visited the project at a time (the end of the first year) when the project team was still exploring the concepts involved and using terms such as 'rehearsal' and 'preparatory work' to refer to the pre-task – thus: 'The aim of the preparatory work is to ensure (i) that the task to be set will, when set, be clearly perceived by learners and (ii) that strategies for tackling the task, as well as the language that will be needed for the purpose, will, when needed, be available for recall and reapplication. In most cases, such preparation is best done through one or more small-scale rehearsals of the task to be presented. The relationship between rehearsal and task is an important means of regulating the challenge of a task; the closer the rehearsal is to the task (in form as well as in substance), the lower the challenge of the latter. In general, no task should be just a duplication of the rehearsal, thus reducing the challenge to a matter of mere recall and reproduction: the task should involve at least a reapplication of the strategies involved to a different situation/set of facts and, at most, an extension (amounting to guided discovery) of the strategies called for.' (RIE Newsletter 1/4, April 1980). Johnson was, of course, also making a prediction about such rehearsing eventually leading to a 'heavy pre-teaching' of language items while the project in reality went on to develop the concept of the pre-task as a parallel task. See also Greenwood (1985) for a misinterpretation of the pre-task, based partly on Johnson's statement and partly on the project's 1980 statement just cited. See also note 16 below.

14 Brumfit's (1984b: 237–8) comments on such marking indicate

an assumption on his part that the marks were meant to be a form of evidence to the public on the success of the project. The project team included the marks in its lesson reports only as rough evidence on the success of the task concerned (within the assumptions of the project and as judged by the project teacher), which is not the same thing as evidence on the project's success. However, such marks can perhaps be a form of evidence on the learner's progress if the relative complexity of the tasks used at different points of time is assessed and, equally, if a subjective uniformity (as a substitute for explicit objectivity) to the teacher's marking is assumed. See Saraswathi (1984) for such a study.

15 The project team's thoughts at the time on language control were: 'The classroom activities we envisage will not be constrained by linguistic control of the kind associated with the structural approach. . . . This does not mean that there will be a total absence of linguistic control in our experimental teaching. Some form of overall control will undoubtedly be necessary in conducting the classroom activities we are thinking of. . . . The actual general control that a teacher needs to maintain will, we think, be determined by the classroom evidence he sees and by trial and error' (RIE Newsletter 1/1, July 1979). And, at the end of the first year's teaching: 'The teacher is to control his language in the classroom in the same way that an adult controls his language in conversing with a child, namely, by avoiding what he considers to be beyond his audience, by glossing, rephrasing, explaining or ascertaining the understanding of such expressions and modifying his assumptions about what is within or beyond his audience's competence, continually in the light of ongoing (interactional) evidence' (RIE Newsletter 1/4 April, 1980).

16 RIE (1980a), RIE (1980b), and RIE (1981) are reports on two of these seminars.

17 This particular lesson, on railway timetables, was one of four subjected to a study at the University of Lancaster, to see if there was any evidence in the classroom discourse of deliberate teaching of language items. Briefly, the tasks used in four of the project lessons in India were used by a British teacher with a class of British children (younger than the class in India) as lessons on the subject-content of the tasks concerned, and audio

transcripts of the resulting lessons in Britain were compared with corresponding transcripts of the lessons in India. None of the differences between the two sets of transcripts indicated any overt or covert teaching of pre-selected language in project teaching. See Collingham (1981), Gilpin (1981), Kumaravadivelu (1981), and Mizon (1981).

18 As indicated by the list, the particular task which Brumfit (1984a, 1984b) uses to illustrate project teaching happens to be an untypical one.

3 Teaching

In Chapter 2 an attempt was made to indicate how the principles and procedures of task-based teaching arose at a certain stage of the project. The purpose of this chapter is to state what further understanding of such teaching was gained in the course of subsequent experience. What is stated here does not therefore constitute a strict description of all the teaching done, but rather an interpretation of the pattern of teaching which came to predominate and was felt to be of particular value.

Reasoning-gap activity

It is necessary first to clarify the sense of the term 'task' for the purpose of this discussion. Meaning-focused activity in the classroom can be divided broadly into three types.

1 *Information-gap activity*, which involves a transfer of given information from one person to another – or from one form to another, or from one place to another – generally calling for the decoding or encoding of information from or into language.[1] One example is pair work in which each member of the pair has a part of the total information (for example an incomplete picture) and attempts to convey it verbally to the other. Another example is completing a tabular representation with information available in a given piece of text. The activity often involves selection of relevant information as well, and learners may have to meet criteria of completeness and correctness in making the transfer.

2 *Reasoning-gap activity*, which involves deriving some new information from given information through processes of inference, deduction, practical reasoning, or a perception of relationships or patterns. One example is working out a teacher's timetable on the basis of given class timetables. Another is deciding what course of action is best (for example cheapest or quickest) for a given purpose and within given constraints. The activity necessarily involves comprehending and conveying information, as in information-gap activity, but the information to be conveyed is not identical with that initially comprehended. There is a piece of reasoning which connects the two.

3 *Opinion-gap activity*, which involves identifying and articulating a personal preference, feeling, or attitude in response to a given situation. One example is story completion; another is taking part in the discussion of a social issue. The activity may involve using factual information and formulating arguments to justify one's opinion, but there is no objective procedure for demonstrating outcomes as right or wrong, and no reason to expect the same outcome from different individuals or on different occasions.

Teaching on the project started with a preference for opinion-gap activity (as being the most likely to ensure a preoccupation with meaning) but soon moved to information-gap and reasoning-gap activities. Between the latter two, a preference for reasoning-gap activity developed gradually, although information-gap activity continued to be used (for example instructions to draw) from time to time. In particular, information-gap activity was seen as a useful preliminary to reasoning-gap activity, either within a task sequence spanning several lessons or in a sequence of questions/exchanges within a single lesson. The first tasks on a new body of information (for example a map or a set of rules) were usually restricted to an interpretation of the information, as a preliminary to tasks which involved inference, deduction, or application to given cases.

Overall, it was reasoning-gap activity which proved to be the most satisfying in the classroom, and the discussion which follows is concerned with possible reasons why. The term 'task' will be used to refer generally to reasoning-gap activity and will also be used to refer to the activity in a lesson as a whole, including 'pre-task' work, unless indicated otherwise.

A pedagogic difficulty with opinion-gap activity is that it is open-ended in its outcomes, in comparison with the other two types which permit agreed decisions about right or wrong outcomes. The knowledge that there is a right answer, and a knowledge of the criterion by which its rightness is to be assessed, provide a sense of security to learners and support their efforts to arrive at answers. This sense of security is important when learners generally feel insecure about the language in which the activity is taking place. Further, objective criteria of rightness and wrongness enable some learners to benefit from the outcomes of other learners' efforts: conclusions can be drawn about right or wrong outcomes from seeing what other outcomes are assessed as right and wrong; and such conclusions can lead to a perception of the right procedures for arriving at outcomes.

Inferencing of this kind is much more difficult in an open-ended activity where there are no decisions on the rightness of outcomes to be used in deducing procedures and, indeed, no logical connections to be established between the problem faced and the procedure adopted. The value of open-ended activity for linguistic development can perhaps be realized better with advanced level learners in a second language (and its value in personal development can no doubt be realized well in mother-tongue instruction) but in the early stages of second language learning, open-ended activity too often leads only to learners' verbal imitation of one another, or of the teacher, and thus ceases to be genuinely open-ended.

Information-gap activity generally takes the form of a one-step procedure – from content to linguistic formulation, or vice versa – for each piece of information to be transferred. It is true that this single step often involves trial and error, thus bringing in criteria of success or adequacy, and it may also involve decisions on the selection of information to be transferred, thus bringing in criteria of relevance. However, such processes involve little negotiation, if negotiation is understood as moving up and down a given line of thought or logic. In contrast, reasoning-gap activity does call for negotiation in this sense since there is in such activity (1) a gap in thought to be bridged, and (2) shared constraints (of practical reasoning, arithmetic, or rules applicable to the activity concerned) on how it is bridged.

Reasoning brings about a more sustained preoccupation with meaning than information transfer does on its own, since it involves deriving one piece of information from another ('working things out' in the mind), not just encoding or decoding given information.[2] More importantly, when a reasoning-gap activity proves difficult for learners, the teacher is able to guide their efforts step by step, making the reasoning explicit or breaking it down into smaller steps, or offering parallel instances to particular steps, as noted in the last chapter. The interaction resulting from this is a public, dialogic expression of the 'working out' which learners have found difficult to do on their own and which, as a result of such expression, they are likely to be able to do more independently (and internally) in a subsequent task or step.[3] Dialogic reasoning is also a process in which the meaning-content of any given exchange is partly predictable and partly unpredictable – predictable because there is a shared perception of purpose and general direction, and unpredictable because the specific meaning-content of any exchange is determined by the outcome of the preceding exchange. The predictability acts as a support to learners' participation in the interaction, while the unpredictability ensures a continual pre-occupation with meaning.

In contrast to the negotiation involved in reasoning-gap activity, interaction in the context of an information-gap activity is likely to be repetitious rather than developmental, thus lowering the level of unpredictability. Interaction in an opinion-gap activity, on the other hand, is likely to have too high a level of unpredictability, thus making it difficult for learners to cope.

There is a sense in which meaning is perceived as one's own when one has, or sees oneself as having, arrived at it oneself; and there is a sense of pleasure in attempting to articulate one's own meaning. There is, however, also a sense of diffidence – and a fear of exposure – in trying to express meaning which is one's own. In general, information-gap activity involves learners in stating meaning which is given to them, though perhaps in a form different from the one in which it is to be stated; it does not involve, or is not seen to involve, stating leaners' own meaning. This is safer but less pleasurable than if the meaning were seen to be one's own.[4] Opinion-gap activity, on the other hand, involves stating meaning which is very much one's own – and of a kind (for example feeling or attitude) which is neither well-defined nor easy to articulate. This leads to a high level of uncertainty, diffidence, or anxiety, though it offers a correspondingly high level of pleasure from success. Reasoning-gap activity seems to offer a balance between these two contradictory tendencies; some meaning is derived from given meaning and what one has derived is, to that extent, one's own; it is, however, only derived from given meaning and is, moreover, objective in character, not a laying bare of one's 'inner thoughts'. There is, as a result, both a measure of satisfaction and a measure of security in attempting to state such meaning.[5]

There appears to be a similar sense in which the language one uses is looked on as one's own or 'borrowed' (i.e. available from an outside source and made use of for a temporary purpose). When learners are dealing with meaning which is given (as in information-gap activity), they tend to look for language which is given as well – and, more importantly, to look on the language they use as being borrowed. If the meaning is not one's own, it seems to follow that the language is not one's own either. Opinion-gap activity, in contrast, calls for both meaning and language which is one's own, and for that reason can seem daunting. It is, in addition, easier to borrow language for objective meaning than it is for subjective meaning.

Reasoning-gap offers opportunities for formulating meaning which is one's own in the sense outlined above – i.e. one has arrived at it oneself – with the possibility of borrowing language, when necessary, for effecting the formulation. More importantly, borrowed language tends to be regarded as one's own to the extent it is used to formulate one's own meaning.

It is possible to think of language being used, in a reasoning-gap activity, either for presentation (i.e. for stating outcomes) or for operation (i.e. for arriving at outcomes; for doing the pieces of reasoning involved) and this has a bearing on the concept of borrowed language becoming one's own. The use of borrowed language is more conscious and deliberate in the context of presentation than it is in the context of operation. There is a more distinct shift of attention from meaning-content to linguistic formulation in the process of stating outcomes than there is in the process of doing the reasoning. The reasoning, of course, can – and frequently does – take place in the learner's mother tongue, but with recurrent teacher–class interaction which 'enacts' the process of reasoning publicly. As noted earlier, it is likely to involve the target language gradually and increasingly, drawing not only on reasoning processes but language from the public interaction. Since reasoning brings about a more sustained preoccupation with meaning than a stating of outcomes, the use of borrowed language in operation is less distinct as a process of borrowing and less deliberate than it is in presentation. Consequently, operation is a more powerful context than presentation for producing the effect of borrowed language becoming one's own. (There is no equation implied here between a learner looking on some piece of language as his or her own and the hypothesized phenomenon of sub-conscious acquisition, though it *is* suggested later in this chapter that the former increases the probability of the latter.)

It was noted above that there is a sense of pleasure in stating meaning which is felt to be one's own. However, there is a corresponding sense of frustration in not being able to put across one's meaning, which is a risk for both reasoning-gap activity and opinion-gap activity. The frustration occurs not only in the context of presentation but also in the context of operation, including interaction with the teacher, and it is stronger in proportion to the degree of one's involvement in the activity. Although these are contexts in which language tends to be borrowed, such borrowing is frequently inadequate to support sustained involvement in an activity, especially in the early stages of language learning. The fact that reasoning-gap activity involves logic, arithmetic, and diagrammatic forms is a clear advantage here: logic, arithmetic, and diagrams in tasks act as alternative 'languages' in which some of the thinking can be done. Indeed, it was found necessary to rely deliberately on such alternative 'languages' in designing feasible tasks for learners at very early stages, and valuable to use them at later stages to ease learners' difficulties in processing, deriving, or presenting information.

Both information-gap activity and reasoning-gap activity involve objective meaning-content, in contrast to opinion-gap activity, and both permit, as we have seen, objective criteria for judging outcomes to be right or wrong. This has an effect on what may be called the 'power-structure' of the class.[6] There are, in fact, three parties to the interaction, not two: the teacher, the learners, and the task itself with its own rules. The teacher and the learners are both bound by the rules of the task and the source of authority is, in a limited but real sense, the task not the teacher. Such equality before the rules of the task imposes a common frame of constraints which creates a form of teacher-learner rapport that is not available either when the activity is form-focused and outcomes are assessed in terms of right or wrong linguistic forms, with the authority inevitably lying with the teacher, or when it involves opinion and there is no recognized source of authority on what is right or wrong. Since reasoning-gap activity involves a wider range of shared constraints – those of inferencing and deduction – than information-gap activity, it has a correspondingly richer potential for such teacher-learner rapport.

Pedagogic advantages such as the above explain why the project came to give a clear preference to reasoning-gap activity, though information-gap activity was often used as a stepping-stone to it. The non-use of opinion-gap activity has been commented on as a limitation of the project on the grounds that the affective aspect of learners' personalities was left unengaged.[7] It should be pointed out, first, that a reliance or reasoning-gap activity did not result in an exclusion of situations involving human feelings and motives. Not only were some tasks in the project's teaching based on dialogues and stories, with inferential comprehension as the basis for reasoning-gap work, but tasks frequently involved the application of rules and other constraints, for example those of distance, cost, and time, to particular individuals in particular situations. Nor does normal classroom discourse exclude reference to opinion (e.g. 'What do you think?' 'Do you agree?') or to personal choices, (e.g.

'Do you want to do this?' 'Would you now like a difficult question?'). Secondly, the classroom is in any case a social situation with its friendships, rivalries, self-images and attitudes, which teachers relate to as well as they can and take into consideration in their management procedures. It would, therefore, be wrong to imagine that task-based teaching involves treating learners as mere reasoning machines, and it was not the project's experience that reasoning-gap activity was 'dull' for learners.[8] Learners' involvement and interest were, in fact, the features most noticed by observers in project classrooms in comparison with normal classrooms. What *is* true is (1) that the meaning-content focused on in classroom activity was factual or rational, rather than emotional or attitudinal, and (2) that no procedures were deliberately employed in teaching for the purpose of creating or increasing learners' emotional involvement. This does not imply any denial of value to emotional involvement for language *learning*. What it implies is a recognition of the much greater suitability of rational activity for language *teaching*, in terms such as control and management by the teacher, approximation to the notions and expectations of formal education, levels of learner security and discourse predictability, and replicability – i.e. the fact that the rules and outcomes of reasoning-gap activity are likely to be similar in the hands of different teachers and learners.

It is also possible to raise wider educational questions about the desirability, for learners' personal development, of attention to rational and emotional domains or, within the rational domain, to convergent and divergent thought. I do not, however, think it is legitimate to expect instruction in a second language to mirror, in the meaning-content it employs, the balance of content in education as a whole. The aim of second language teaching, as conceived of on the project, was to develop in learners a grammatical competence in the language, and the procedure thought to be most likely to achieve this was a preoccupation with certain forms of meaning-content. It is reasonable to ask, in view of the fact that second-language instruction was taking place as a part of formal education as a whole, whether the meaning-content employed was compatible with that of formal education, and there is clearly no incompatibility between convergent thought (which reasoning-gap activity relies on) and educational content. It is perhaps more reasonable, as suggested already, to expect courses in the mother tongue, in which the aim is not the development of grammatical competence as such, to consider the needs of learners' growth as individuals in the meaning-content they employ. A related question is whether it is fair to expect all learners to engage in reasoning activity and whether, in particular, learners with aptitudes in other directions, for example divergent thought or artistic activity, might not find themselves at a disadvantage?[9] Again, however, I do not think that task-based teaching makes, or needs to make, any higher demands on reasoning than are made in education in general. All learners in schools are expected to achieve some degree of numeracy and some understanding of science, and educated citizens are expected to understand something of the laws and regulations they are required to conform to.

On the question of aptitude, it needs to be remembered that no equation is implied in task-based teaching between the processes of conscious reasoning which classroom activity demands, and the processes of subconscious language acquisition which such activity brings about.[10] Reasoning activity is proposed as a methodology of language *teaching*, not as a hypothesis about the process of language *learning*. The expectation in task-based teaching is not that success in reasoning activity will in itself represent success in developing grammatical competence; the expectation is, rather, that success in reasoning activity will support sustained engagement in such activity and that sustained engagement is a condition favourable to the development of grammatical competence.[11]

Pre-task and task

As indicated in Chapter 2, the general pattern of each lesson in task-based teaching is that it consists of two tasks of the same kind, one of them to be attempted publicly as a teacher-guided, whole-class activity, and the other to be attempted by learners independently. The two tasks are similar in that they demand similar processes of reasoning, or consist of similar sequences of questions (each sequence graded within itself), and employ either the same or similar situations, sets of facts, or texts. Each task, however, requires an independent effort of the mind, i.e. it is not possible to transfer either the outcome or the procedures of one mechanically to the other. The pattern is roughly analogous to that of a lesson in mathematics, where a problem is worked out publicly and a similar problem is then set for learners to work out on their own.

The term 'pre-task' refers, as noted earlier, to the task to be attempted publicly while the term 'task' refers to what learners are to attempt on their own. This discussion is concerned with the advantages of organizing lessons on a pre-task and task pattern. The pre-task is a context in which any difficulties which learners may have in understanding the nature of the activity – seeing what information is given, what needs to be done, and what constraints apply – are revealed and the teacher is able to provide appropriate assistance, perhaps by paraphrasing or glossing expressions, by employing parallel situations or diagrams, or by reorganizing information. In this sense, the pre-task is preparation for the task, since learners are less likely, while engaged later in a similar activity on their own, to fail to see what is given and what needs to be done.

The pre-task is also a context in which learners' difficulties in carrying out the required reasoning are revealed and the teacher is able, in response, to engage in appropriate interaction, breaking down the effort needed into smaller steps and, in the process, making public the procedures to be employed. Since the difficulties of learners in any class are varied, in degree as well as in kind, the teacher's interaction with several learners at different points of the pre-task helps to ensure that the class as a whole receives a public demonstration of all or most of what is to be done. The work is not, however, done or seen as merely a demonstration: it is a task in its own right, with various parts of it being attempted publicly by different members of the class and with the outcomes of those attempts being examined and shown to be right or wrong. The learners who make such public attempts are generally the more extrovert or adventurous ones, who are willing to take risks in front of their peers, or the more capable ones, who feel sufficiently confident of success. There are others in the class who are less extrovert or less confident and who therefore prefer to work things out by watching others' attempts while not being on trial themselves. Some of them feel sufficiently confident, after some watching and working out, to make a public attempt and the teacher is able, with some experience, to sense which learners are close to that stage and to invite or encourage them to join in. It is not, however, the aim of the pre-task to ensure a public attempt by every learner, and it is normally about half the class, or less, who participate overtly at this stage. The pre-task as a whole-class activity is thus an opportunity for some learners to learn by making an attempt, and equally an opportunity for others to learn without taking the risk of public failure. What motivates the learning by observation is not only the possibility that observation may lead to a level of confidence which later makes public participation possible but, more immediately, the knowledge that there is going to be a similar task to attempt individually in a short while, at which one can succeed on the strength of one's observation at this stage. The task therefore motivates attention to the pre-task, just as the pre-task facilitates the task by acting as a public demonstration.

The pre-task enables the teacher to assess how difficult or easy the task which is to follow is going to be for the class and, within limits, to adjust its difficulty-level accordingly. For instance a part of the task which calls for complex reasoning may be left out; alternatively, points of anticipated difficulty may be highlighted by the use of additional parallel questions, or explicit and detailed treatment of the reasoning processes involved. When, later, learners have attempted the task, their performance on it, as revealed in the course of the marking, acts as an indication of the level of difficulty at which the pre-task and task in the next lesson should be set and, in particular, what kinds of difficulty need to be highlighted in the next pre-task. The pre-task is therefore an occasion for making use of the evidence from learners' performance on the preceding task as well as for anticipating and easing learners' difficulty on the task to follow.

The language which the teacher employs in the classroom, both in presenting the information relevant to the task and in conducting the interaction, is (1) what the activity concerned calls for and (2) what the teacher considers likely to be comprehended by the class in the context of that activity. The teacher, however, needs evidence during the course of the activity on whether or not the language is being comprehended adequately by the class; and the form of discourse which the pre-task produces (i.e. a pedagogic dialogue) makes such evidence continually available, enabling the teacher to adapt and adjust his or her language accordingly. In general, the nature of the pre-task helps to ensure that the language needed for the activity is employed in the classroom at a level of complexity which is manageable for the class.

Finally, the pre-task and task pattern divides a lesson desirably into an initial period of whole-class activity, teacher-direction, and oral interaction, and a later period of sustained self-dependent effort by learners.

Reasonable challenge

Learners' immediate motivation in the task-based classroom derives from the intellectual pleasure of solving problems, in addition to such traditional sources as a desire to do well at school, to win the approval of the teacher, or to gain the admiration of one's peers. Although what is important for language learning is learners' engagement in a task rather than their success in it, some measure of success is essential for maintaining learners' desire to make the effort, as repeated failure can lead to a sense of frustration or a negative self-image. It is therefore important for the teacher to regulate the challenge offered by tasks and operate generally with some notion of what represents reasonable challenge for a given class. The concept of reasonable challenge implies that learners should not be able to meet the challenge too easily but *should* be able to meet it with some effort.[12] This is not just a matter of the teacher's assessment of the learners' ability; it is a matter of the learners' own perceptions, too. If a task looks very easy to learners, they expect no sense of achievement from success in it and are likely to be less than keen to attempt it. If, on the other hand, the task looks so difficult that they feel sure they will fail in it, they are likely to be reluctant to make an effort at all. A task should, ideally, look difficult but attainable to learners. The effort learners put into a given task may also be influenced by such additional factors as comparison or rivalry with their peers, and whether or not they feel that the teacher thinks them capable of success.

Learners in a class, of course, vary in their abilities as well as their perceptions, and the teacher can only hope to adjust the level of challenge to suit the largest possible number. The fact that tasks are normally organized as a series of graded and parallel questions is of some help: different questions prove reasonably challenging to different learners and a parallel question proves reasonably challenging to some learners who have already watched a similar question being answered by other learners. The teacher is also able to assist in regulating the challenge by means of techniques such as negotiation and simplification, and to be guided by continual feedback from learners in the course of the pre-task. Nevertheless, the teacher needs a workable criterion for assessing the reasonableness of the challenge of tasks for a given class; and the learners' performance on the 'task' (the individual activity) in each lesson provides a useful basis. Teachers on the project used the working rule that the challenge of a task was reasonable if approximately half the learners in the class were successful on approximately half the task (as shown by a marking of their work). This, of course, leaves open the possibility that some learners consistently find the tasks too difficult while some others find them too easy, but a review of learners' performance over a stretch of time showed that this was true only of a small number (about 10 per cent of the class at each end). Many learners seemed to perform differently, relative to each other, on different task-types, such as those involving inferencing, or counting, or spatial or directional concepts, and some appeared to perform differently at different points on a task-sequence of increasing complexity.

The working rule for reasonable challenge was the outcome of experience and proved to be adequate as a means of monitoring learners' success on tasks in that there was, after the project's first year, no noticeable sagging of morale in any of the project classes. The monitoring also brought to light the fact that there is an optimal length to task sequences: when tasks of the same type were set in successive lessons in an order of increasing complexity, the success rate normally increased from day to day, probably as a result of an increase in familiarity with the task-type concerned. However, learners' success began to decline after a certain number of lessons (five or six for most task-types), although the gradation in the sequence of tasks had not become perceptibly steeper. In keeping with the interpretation that the initial increase in success was due to familiarity with the task-type, one can attribute the later decline to over-familiarity resulting in a form of 'fatigue'. As a result of this observation, teaching on the project introduced a regular change of task-types after every few lessons, different ones thus being used cyclically. There was no indication of any 'fatigue' when a task-type was taken up again after one or more other task-sequences had intervened.

Teacher's language

In planning a task for any lesson, the teacher considered, among other things, whether it would be possible to set that task in language simple enough for the class to understand. This assessment could only be a rough one and typically involved decisions about what terms to use to refer to particular objects or concepts (for example 'fare' or 'cost'? 'continue' or 'take forward'?), which were central to the task. There were also decisions about how to word particular questions in order to control the complexity of the inferencing they required. Then, in the classroom, the teacher controlled the complexity of his or her language in more or less the same way as an adult does in speaking to a child – avoiding or paraphrasing what he or she felt might be too difficult, repeating statements, and speaking slowly when there seemed to be difficulties of understanding.[13]

Such *ad hoc* simplification worked in the project classrooms for the same reasons that it does elsewhere: first, the purpose of language use was to get some meaning-content across, and there was an inherent connectedness and coherence to the meaning-content being put across at different points, making expectations possible; secondly, there was a criterion of adequacy for the comprehension being aimed at (i.e. enough to get on with the task); and thirdly, there was continual evidence available on whether or not enough comprehension was in fact being achieved from the learners' participation in the pedagogic dialogue. No attempt was made by the teacher to ensure that all the language which he or she used was understood by learners: it was assumed, indeed, that some or much of the language made only a peripheral impression and some of it went unregistered. Nor was it assumed that such comprehension as took place represented 'full' comprehension of the samples of language concerned. There is, in fact, no identifiable sense in which any sample of language can be said to have been comprehended 'fully' by anyone.[14] Comprehension can only be viewed as being adequate or inadequate for given purposes, and is typically paid attention to when it has been inadequate. Further, the existence of purposes and criteria of adequacy not only help to make evidence of comprehension available, but act as an aid to the process of comprehension, by delimiting the range of possible meanings and making trial and error possible. (One of the weaknesses of the S-O-S teaching procedure which attempts to present pieces of language 'meaningfully' is that the teacher has to assume blindly that the degree of comprehension is proportionate to his effort in presentation – or seek, unreasonably, an assessment from learners with questions like 'Do you understand?').[15]

It is common to look on linguistic syllabuses as a means, among other things, of delimiting the language to be employed in the classroom at any given time – a means of protecting the learner from the bewilderment of facing too much language. But task-based activity has the effect of delimiting language too, and in a way which is more natural in the sense that the delimitation of language results from a delimitation of meaning-content in the form of tasks. The language that is employed in task-based activity is 'free' (i.e. constrained only by the needs of the activity and on-the-spot feasibility, not by any predetermined linguistic progression or preselection) but it is neither unlimited nor unmanageably complex, thanks to the nature of the activity itself.[16] In addition, the devices developed to facilitate a preoccupation with meaning, such as the organization of the activity into pre-task and task, and the use of task sequences and parallel questions, have the effect of bringing about a measure of recurrence, within and across lessons, of particular forms of language in response to need and without specific planning. This is, of course, the case with any recurrent real-life event, for example lectures on the same subject, or buying and selling. If the term 'repetition' can be restricted to refer to occurrences which are planned and deliberate, it is possible to say that task-based activity does not employ repetition but, by its nature, brings about a measure of recurrence. Recurrent language is meaning-focused, since it is brought about by the needs of meaning-content and, given the perception that the form of language is best learnt when the learner's attention is focused on meaning, repetition does not have the same value for learning as recurrence.

Learners' language

Learners' use of language in task-based activity was a matter of their coping as well as they could. They adopted various strategies such as using single words, resorting to gestures, quoting from the blackboard or the sheet which stated the task, waiting for the teacher to formulate alternative responses so that they could simply choose one of them, seeking a suggestion from a peer or, as a last resort, using the mother tongue. Tasks for learners in early stages were so formulated that they could convey the outcome of their individual work in non-linguistic forms such as numbers, letters of the alphabet, and diagrams. However, even with this kind of task, interaction at the pre-task stage called for verbal communication. Since responses were (and were seen to be) assessed only for their content, learners' concern in making those responses was to get meaning-content across as clearly as possible. The teacher helped by means of techniques such as offering alternative responses for the learner to choose from (which, incidentally, is not just a means of reducing learners' difficulty in verbalization but a means of clarifying the meaning-content of the problem and guiding thought as well), expanding inadequately formulated responses, and articulating a response ambivalently signalled by a learner then seeking the learner's confirmation of the interpretation made. The general understanding which prevailed in the classroom was that the learners had to meet the challenge of the task and, if they were unable to state an outcome or response adequately, they had a right to draw on the teacher's knowledge of the language. It was, that is to say, an instance of defeat if learners were unable to do the thinking, but not if they were unable to say what they wanted to say in the way some other learners or the teacher could. Although tasks were presented and carried out in the target language, the use of the learner's mother tongue in the classroom was neither disallowed nor excluded. The teacher normally used it only for an occasional glossing of words or for some complex procedural instructions, for example: 'Leave the rest of the page blank in your notebooks and go on to the next page, for the next question'. Learners' use of the mother tongue in all project classes revealed a shared notion among them of what may be called 'public' and 'private' discourse. Learners refrained from speaking to the teacher in the mother tongue (except as a last resort and with considerable reluctance) in whole-class activity when the teacher was in front of the class but felt much freer to do so at the individual task stage when the teacher was going round the class and the learner was therefore consulting the teacher 'privately' or, at the pre-task stage, when the learner happened to be at the blackboard and close to the teacher, which made it 'private' talk as well.

Reference was made above to learners quoting from what was written on the blackboard or from the statement of a task on paper, as a means of finding words in which to put their answers: discussion earlier referred to the same phenomenon as 'borrowing' language. It is perhaps useful here to distinguish, in considering learners' use of the target language, between 'production', 'borrowing', and 'reproduction' as follows. Production is self-initiated verbal formulation, resulting from a deployment of linguistic competence. It is automatic, that is it occurs while attention remains on the meaning-content the language expresses, and can be thought of as having been generated by an internal grammar to match some self-initiated meaning-content. Borrowing, in contrast, is taking over an available verbal formulation in order to express some self-initiated meaning-content, instead of generating the formulation from one's own competence – a matter of saying what one wants to say in someone else's words. It is not automatic but deliberate, i.e. there is a shift of attention from meaning-content to language itself and a conscious decision about what available formulation to select. The decision, however, is one's own, and the purpose is seen as one of expressing meaning-content, not borrowing as an end in itself. Reproduction is different from both production and borrowing in that its purpose is, wholly or partly, to take over an available sample of language and the decision to do so is not one's own but made in compliance with the requirement or expectation of the teacher. It is a deliberate act in which the attention is either entirely on language, or alternates between language and meaning-content. Both language and meaning-content are seen as 'borrowed' and, in the case of the latter, this is so even if the learner needs to change it in some way before matching it with borrowed language. These distinctions are set out in tabular form below.

	Production	Borrowing	Reproduction
Meaning-content	Self-initiated	Self-initiated	Taken over
Verbal formulation	Self-initiated	Taken over	Taken over
Decision to 'take over'	(Not relevant)	Internal	External
Linguistic competence	Deployed	Not deployed	Not deployed

Table 2 *Distinctions between production, borrowing, and reproduction*

From the perspective which informs task-based teaching, reproduction is of little value to language acquisition. In contrast, production is of value both in furthering acquisition and as evidence of it. Borrowing is necessary for maintaining task-based activity (and thereby a meaning-focused condition which is of value to acquisition) and is probably also of some direct value to acquisition. Both acquisition and production will be commented on further in the next chapter.

Incidental correction

As mentioned above, teachers expanded and articulated learners' responses in the course of the pedagogic dialogues that took place in project classrooms. In doing so, they also replaced any grammatically incorrect forms in learners' expressions with correct ones. They restated learners' responses, that is to say, in the way that they, the teachers, would state them – more fully as well as more correctly. When different learners wrote things on the blackboard in the course of the pre-task, they felt free to ask the teacher or fellow-learners to spell particular words for them or to suggest ways of continuing or completing what they were writing; and when spelling errors were made, other learners pointed them out if they noticed them and, if not, the teachers drew attention to them, or set them right themselves. Learners were rarely able to point out errors of grammar but they were aware that there were likely to be deficiencies other than spelling in what they wrote on the blackboard and expected the teachers to set them right, just as they did in oral interaction. The teachers made the correction on the blackboard, or told the learner who was writing what to change, but did not attempt to follow up an error with an explanation or other examples of the same kind. When the teachers marked learners' responses to the task (i.e. the outcome of individual work), they corrected the language in the same way as they did on the blackboard, though (1) the marking itself was done for content, as noted earlier, and (2) for want of time the language repair was much less complete and consistent than on the blackboard, and sometimes not possible at all. When the work was handed back to learners at the beginning of the next lesson, they looked to see what mark they had received and tried to work out why the responses marked wrong (for content) were wrong, often looking at some fellow-learner's responses and how they were marked. There is no evidence on what effect, if any, the linguistic correction of responses had, but there is some evidence that, when the next day's 'task' was of the same type (i.e. within the same task-sequence), some learners looked back, in the process of finding a way of stating some response, to the way they had stated a similar response the previous day and used it as a source to borrow from.

It seems useful to call such language repair 'incidental correction', and to distinguish it from 'systematic correction' which involves a larger interruption of ongoing activity to focus learners' attention on an error that has taken place by providing an explanation or a set of other such instances in the hope of preventing a recurrence of the error.[17] Systematic correction also involves making the errors noticed in one lesson the basis of some planned work in the classroom in a subsequent lesson, or anticipating particular types of error and taking some preventive action. It includes consistently correcting errors in learners' written work and marking the work itself, wholly or partly, for linguistic accuracy. Incidental correction, by contrast, is (1) confined to particular 'tokens' (i.e. the error itself is corrected, but there is no generalization to the type of error it represents), (2) only responsive (i.e. not leading to any preventive or pre-emptive action), (3) facilitative (i.e. regarded by learners as a part of getting on with the activity in hand, not as a separate objective and not as being more important than other aspects of the activity), and (4) transitory (i.e. drawing attention to itself only for a moment – not for as long as systematic correction does). There is evidently a great deal which is not yet understood about the role and value of correction; and incidental correction in project teaching was largely a matter of following unclear pedagogic instincts, attempting not to miss opportunities for making available relevant samples of language to learners but, at the same time, taking care to exclude any sustained attention to language itself which would have resulted in a reduction in the focus on meaning.

Notes

1 See Johnson (1982: 163–75). I am using the term 'information-gap' in a more restricted sense than Johnson's. Since Johnson does not make the three-way distinction I am making, 'information-gap' would for him presumably include any or all of the three types.

2 Where the purpose of teaching is to enable learners to conform to social conventions in language use rather than to develop an internal grammatical competence, the verbal encoding and decoding involved in information-gap activity is perhaps of some special value.

3 Vigotsky's view of the development of reasoning in children seems to support the conjecture made here on the strength of classroom experience. See Vigotsky (1978: 56–7): 'An operation that initially represents an external activity is reconstructed and begins to occur internally. . . . An interpersonal process is transformed into an intrapersonal one.' See also Frawley and Lantolf (1985: 20–21) who provide an interpretation of Vigotsky's perception of this phenomenon: 'All human beings as children are initially integrated into the strategic process of reasoning through social interaction, between the self and a more experienced member of a culture, either an adult or an older peer who is capable of strategic reasoning. . . . The transition from inter- to intrapsychological reasoning through mediation, as we said earlier, is a dialogic process, a process in

which an adult undertakes to direct a child through a task, and where the child provides feedback to the adult, who then makes the necessary adjustments in the kind of direction offered to the child.' See also Donaldson (1978) for a view of the centrality of inferencing in first language development.

4 The fact that learners generally do not regard mere repetition in the language classroom as serious activity and tend to carry it out, when asked to, with a sense of resentment or condescension or frivolity, is perhaps due to the fact that no meaning seen as their own is being expressed. This may also explain why, when meaning-content is strictly specified for a piece of 'guided composition' as a means of keeping the writing within the limits of the language to be practised, learners seem perversely to deviate from the content specified, thus producing unpredicted errors of language. When, at the other end of the scale of control, 'free' composition is attempted by asking learners to state their own attitudes and feelings towards a topic, they tend to take stereotypic stances as masks, thus hiding their actual attitudes, probably from a sense of insecurity and a fear of exposure.

5 There may be a case for moving generally from information-gap to reasoning-gap to opinion-gap activity as learners progress in their language acquisition, though genuine opinion-gap activity is likely to be feasible only at very advanced stages, and may have to be analysed further into more and less feasible areas of content.

6 See Brumfit's (1984a: 56) description of what he regards as fluency activity: 'Students should not normally be aware of intervention by the teacher as teacher rather than as communicator during the performance of the activity. This has implications for the power relations in the class.'

7 See, for instance, Brumfit (1984b).

8 See Greenwood (1985: 271): 'One wonders whether life consists of anything other than maps and plans for these Bangalore learners.' Greenwood admits that he is speaking from limited knowledge of the project, but it is true enough that a large number of the tasks used have to do with maps and plans. What I find interesting is Greenwood's equation of the second language classroom with 'life'. One would presumably

not ask, in examining a course in science, whether 'life' consists for the students concerned of anything other than material facts or, in examining a course in history, of anything other than dates and names from the past: one recognizes that whatever else life should consist of for learners might well be available elsewhere in the curriculum. Within second language teaching, it is quite possible to ask, of structurally graded courses, whether life for learners should not go beyond vocabulary and structural patterns; and, of courses which use the 'human' content of stories, poems, and personal anecdotes, whether life should not go beyond fiction and subjectivity.

9 See Brumfit (1984b).

10 The implications of studies of the 'good language learner' (e.g. Rubin 1975; Naiman *et al.* 1978) for the pedagogic perspective being presented here are not clear. If success in first language learning is independent of differences between individuals, and if second language learning involves essentially the same processes as first language learning (a hypothesis inherent in the thinking on the project), then differences in personalities or strategies can only be relevant as the conditions, in some sense, in which language learning takes place, not as the processes of language learning as such. The project was concerned with exploring just one condition of learning which it considered central, namely a preoccupation with meaning, and a contingent struggle with language. There may be other conditions which are important as well, though there is a prior question, in considering such other conditions, of what concept of 'knowing a language' one is operating with. Also, in a pedagogic enquiry, one is looking for conditions which can be created or influenced by procedures of teaching. If, for instance, some personality factors turned out to be relevant conditions, pedagogy would have to choose between attempting to alter some learners' personalities and leaving learners to learn the language as well as their personalities permit.

11 There are, of course, problems arising from this view in deciding what constitutes evidence of success in developing grammatical competence, which is not indicated simply by success in doing tasks, but manifests itself nevertheless in a meaning-focused context.

12 Vigotsky's concept of the 'zone of proximal development'

seems to lend some support. See Vigotsky (1978: 86): 'The zone of proximal development is the distance between the actual development stage as determined by independent problem solving and the level of potential development as determined through problem solving under adult guidance or in collaboration with more capable peers.'

13 The procedures are generally those which have been studied under the label 'caretaker talk'. See Corder (1981) for a discussion and further references.

14 'Comprehensible input' (Krashen 1981, 1982; Krashen and Terrell, 1983) is therefore an inadequate concept for language pedagogy. Comprehensibility is not an attribute of some sample of language in relation to some learner: a crucial third factor is a criterion of adequacy, i.e. the level of comprehension needed for a given purpose. The same sample of language can be comprehensible to the same learner at one level and for one purpose, and incomprehensible at another. Teaching is, therefore, primarily a matter of regulating the level of comprehension needed (by setting up goals and criteria of success and failure) and only secondarily a matter of doing things to the input – for example simplifying it – to assist the learner in achieving that level.

There is a similar difficulty with Krashen's concept of 'i + 1'. Given that input to the learner is not to be graded grammatically (a point on which the project's position is identical with Krashen's), there is little use which teaching can make of the i + 1 concept. What teaching *can* do is to ensure that the learner has a reason (and, as far as possible, a desire) to process input and that the purpose goes on increasing in complexity at such a pace that it remains, at any given point, difficult but attainable. This is the concept of reasonable challenge in tasks. See also Note 15 below.

15 A concentration on making language easy for learners to understand also runs the risk of making understanding so easy that little effort is called for from the learner and, as a result, little learning takes place. As Vigotsky (1978: 89) points out, 'learning which is oriented toward developmental stages that have already been reached is ineffective . . . the only "good learning" is that which is an advance of development.' See also Palmer (1921: 91): 'There is an immense difference between

difficult work and bewildering work; of difficulties there must necessarily be many, but of bewilderment there should be none.' Presenting language comprehensibly but without a purpose to the comprehension can remove difficulty and create bewilderment.

16 There are English-medium schools in India in which all subjects are taught in English. There is, of course, no linguistic syllabus for any subject other than English itself, and yet the language used in all classrooms gets limited and regulated as well as increasingly complex as learners move into higher classes. Teachers of history, science, etc., who are not trained as teachers of English, all simplify their language to the extent demanded by their classes for an understanding of what is being taught.

17 Some correction of language takes place in all classrooms in English-medium schools, but the teachers of other subjects do not regard the activity as teaching English, only as paying what attention needs to be paid to English in order to get on with the teaching of the subject in question. Students' work is, of course, marked only for subject-content. The kinds of correction which other teachers make in such schools relates to the kinds of correction which teachers of English make, in the same schools, in roughly the way 'incidental correction' relates to 'systematic correction'.

4 Learning

This chapter attempts to state how task-based teaching of the kind already discussed was perceived on the project to lead to language learning, and why any systematicity in teaching in terms of language structure was thought to be of little value to the process of learning. Some of the project's ideas on these issues were outlined in Chapter 2; what follows is an elaboration of those ideas, indicating ways in which they developed further during the course of the project. Second language acquisition is an area in which a great deal of research has taken place in recent years but the project's ideas, though similar in many ways to those arising from this research, for the most part developed independently, and in the context of an exploration of language teaching rather than directly of language learning.[1] Any retrospective attempt to relate, in any detail, these two sets of ideas would distort the intended focus of this account. The purpose of what follows therefore is confined to indicating what concepts of language learning lay behind the teaching procedures developed on the project, and how those concepts clarified and articulated themselves in the process of developing and discussing the procedures.

Linguistic competence

As noted earlier, although learners' preoccupation with tasks was perceived on the project to bring about the development of linguistic competence, their ability to do tasks successfully was not taken to be identical or co-extensive with linguistic competence as such. Success in doing tasks involves more than linguistic competence in one sense, and less in another. It involves more in that the processes of understanding, thinking, and stating outcomes which are necessary in accomplishing a task are supported by various non-linguistic resources such as those of practical reasoning and numeracy. They are also supported by the way tasks are structured, with a limitation of possible interpretations and outcomes, or with parallel instances. On the other hand, success in doing a task involves less than linguistic competence in that, strictly speaking, language needs to be comprehended only for a certain purpose (hence, to a certain degree) and an outcome needs to be formulated in language only to the extent necessary for putting its meaning-content across. Now, linguistic competence involves not just being able to communicate meaning but, in that process, conforming to linguistic (i.e. grammatical and lexical) norms as well.[2] Although learners in a task-based classroom can get their meaning across by means of ungrammatical expressions, task-based teaching is meant to enable them to achieve, in due course, grammatical conformity in their use of language. Grammatical conformity in language use is thought to arise from the operation of some internal system of abstract rules or principles, and it is the development of that system that task-based activity is intended to promote. While, that is to say, learners are engaged in an effort to understand and express meaning, a process of internal system-development is hypothesized to go on at a subconscious level of their minds. This process of system-building is thought to be activated or furthered by immediate needs to understand and express meaning but, once activated, capable of going beyond what is strictly called for by those immediate needs, achieving grammatical conformity in addition to communication.[3] Learners engaged in task-based activity are, at any given time, meeting the demands made on their understanding and expression by bringing into play such internal systems as they have developed so far (which, being in formative stages, may lead to miscomprehension or ungrammatical expression) but, in doing so, they are also developing those systems a little further. It is in this sense that meaning-focused activity constitutes a condition for language acquisition without success in such activity being identical with language acquisition.

Acquisition and deployment

Meaning-focused activity involves learners in making sense of various pieces of language in the course of understanding the information provided, interpreting the teacher's questions or instructions, working out a solution, or mentally following an exchange between the teacher and a fellow-learner. Each piece of language embodies some meaning-content as well as some elements of language structure: indeed, it embodies meaning-content partly as a result of being linguistically structured. In their efforts to cope with a task, learners thus receive a form of 'intensive exposure' to entities which represent a matching of meaning and structure. Task-based teaching operates with the concept that, while the conscious mind is working out some of the meaning-content, a subconscious part of the mind perceives, abstracts, or acquires (or re-creates, as a cognitive structure) some of the linguistic structuring embodied in those entities, as a step in the development of an internal system of rules.[4] The intensive exposure caused by an effort to work out meaning-content is thus a condition which is favourable to the subconscious abstraction – or cognitive formation – of language structure.

This way of looking at the process of acquisition does not imply that acquisition of any element of language structure is necessarily an instant, one-step procedure. It may take several instances of intensive exposure to different samples of language before any abstraction is made, or cognitive structure formed, and particular instances may or may not lead to any such result. The cognitive structures formed may at first be faint, or incomplete, or inaccurate, becoming better defined with further exposure, or with the formation of some other structures which have a bearing on them. Also, different learners in a class may, in the course of the same classroom activity, be preoccupied with different pieces of language, thus abstracting different structures, or with the same piece of language with different results (i.e. making the abstraction with different degrees of firmness, completeness, or accuracy). Language learning perceived in this way cannot be specifically predicted or controlled by language teaching. Teaching can only hope to increase the probability of such learning.

Meaning-focused activity is of value not only to the initial formation of the internal system but to its further development or elaboration too. The effort to make sense of a piece of language occasions not only a possible 'yield' (i.e. the subconscious abstraction of a structure) but also a corresponding 'investment': the effort draws on such abstract linguistic structures as have been formed already, whether it be firmly or faintly, accurately or inaccurately. Available abstract structures are thus deployed on new (or recurring) samples of language, helping to interpret those samples but, in the process, themselves getting firmed up, modified, extended, or integrated with one another. Recurrent effort at comprehension thus leads to recurrent deployment and to the gradual growth of an internal linguistic competence. Furthermore, deployment occurs not only in the process of comprehension but in the process of production as well; and deployment in production has value for the development of the internal system in that, like comprehension, it results in a firming up of the abstract structures concerned. It is, however, likely that abstract structures need to be formed more firmly for deployment in production than they need to be for comprehension, a hypothesis that will be expanded upon later in this chapter.

System-development

Although acquisition and deployment have been outlined above as different concepts, they are not seen as separate processes in the development of the internal system. Every effort to comprehend or convey meaning involves a deployment of abstract structures that have already been formed, and every instance of deployment constitutes a step in the further development of those structures. The structures deployed may be firmed up or modified, or new structures may be formed as an extension of existing ones. Also, deployment of one piece of language may facilitate abstraction from another. The abstract structures available at any time are likely to be functioning as a related system (as has been argued in the study of interlanguage) rather than discretely; and this means that a modification or extension of one part of the system can have consequences for other parts.[5] Given such a process of system-development, what is abstracted from any piece of language is not just what is occasioned by a working out of its meaning, but what is relevant to some part or other of the developing system itself. This process of system-development is likely to go on until all relevant parts have been abstracted in the course of recurrent deployment.[6] A fully-formed internal system is thus likely to achieve, when deployed thereafter, conformity to the norms of language structure, regardless of the strict needs of meaning-exchange in particular instances.

Deployment is a notion which also applies to the operation of linguistic competence in normal language use. A characteristic of normal language use is that while the user's conscious mind is occupied with the meaning-content that is being exchanged, an internal linguistic competence is operating simultaneously at a less conscious level, both to facilitate this exchange by bringing about a matching of meaning and language structure and to ensure conformity to grammatical norms. Perceptions of this two-level operation in language use have led in the past to notions such as automaticity and 'associative habit' as a means of characterizing the operation of linguistic competence, and to teaching techniques such as 'practice' in various forms ('form-focused' and 'meaningful' activity as characterized in Chapter 2) which address themselves directly to that linguistic level. The perception of a more integral link between the two operations led, on the project, to the notion of deployment and to meaning-focused activity, a form of pedagogy which addresses itself directly to a conscious preoccupation with meaning-content in order to achieve a deployable linguistic competence.

Rule-focused activity

It must be remembered that the reference above to an internal system of rules is not to any particular descriptive or generative grammar produced by linguists. The study of grammar by linguists is an attempt to *discover* various aspects of the internal system, while language pedagogy is an attempt to *develop* that system in learners. As was noted in Chapter 2, linguists' study of grammar has made it abundantly clear that the internal system developed by successful learners is far more complex than any grammar yet constructed by a linguist, and it is therefore unreasonable to suppose that any language learner can acquire a deployable internal system by consciously understanding and assimilating the rules in a linguist's grammar, not to mention those in a 'pedagogic' grammar which represent a simplification of the linguist's grammar and consequently can only be still further removed from the internally developed system. Moreover, although linguists' grammars aim to provide some understanding of the internal system, they cannot, and do not, claim any isomorphism with it in terms of specific correspondence between units, operations, or organization. Linguists construct conceptual models (acting as intellectuals, rather than as language-users), the outputs of which match as closely as possible the output of the internal system shared by language-users. However, output similarity does not justify an assumption of isomorphism, even when output is taken to include 'intuitions' about well-formedness or ambiguity. At best, these intuitions represent expressions of the internal system, not introspections on its form. Furthermore, teaching a descriptive grammar can only be done in some order suggested by its organization, implying the even less plausible assumption of a correspondence between such organizational logic and the developmental sequence of the internal system. Most importantly, teaching a descriptive grammar is likely – as has been pointed out at various times in the history of language pedagogy – to promote in learners an explicit knowledge of that grammar, rather than a deployable internal system.

Planned progression

For similar reasons, the use of a descriptive grammar 'behind the classroom' as a means of regulating teaching through planned progression, preselection, and form-focused activity is also unlikely to be helpful in promoting an internal system. The purpose of using a descriptive grammar in this way (as noted in Chapter 2) is to ensure that learners infer the rules of language structure, one by one, directly from pre-arranged samples made available to them. It is thought that when learners infer rules in this way, they internalize them better than if the rules were taught explicitly. However, the assumption is still that the descriptive grammar used to arrange samples represents the internal system to be constructed by learners. A unit of grammar used as the basis of a set of samples is taken to be a unit of the internal system, and the sequence in which different units are brought into the teaching is taken to be the sequence of internal grammar-construction. Planned linguistic progression in teaching thus involves both an assumption of isomorphism between the descriptive grammar used and the internal system, and an assumption of correspondence between the grammatical progression used in teaching and the developmental sequence of the internal system. In particular, it assumes that the development of the internal system is a discrete item, additive process – an assumption which goes counter to the highly plausible perception in interlanguage studies that the process is a holistic one, consisting of a sequence of transitional systems.[7]

Pre-selection

Pre-selection of particular units of a descriptive grammar for particular lessons arises from planned progression and results in form-focused activity. It aims, on the one hand, to ensure that learners receive, at each stage of the teaching, samples representing the unit of grammar relevant to that stage in the planned progression, and is therefore based on the same assumption of isomorphism, developmental sequence, and additive process. Pre-selection also aims, on the other hand, to ensure that the pre-selected unit of grammar is learnt well by learners in the course of the lesson concerned, by making provision for a good deal of repetition or practice with samples of language representing that unit. The concept of learning which lies behind such repetition and practice, however, conflicts with that which underlies task-based teaching. Practice relies on a focus on form – or focus on nothing in particular, as in the mechanical handling of a given piece of language – and on what may be regarded as the 'quantum' of exposure. In contrast, task-based teaching relies on a focus on meaning and what was referred to above as the 'intensity' of exposure. The two approaches conflict in that planned repetition and practice (unlike unplanned 'recurrence', see pages 58–9) can be employed in the classroom only at the expense of a sustained focus on meaning, and vice versa.[8]

Meaningful practice

What was referred to in Chapter 2 as 'meaningful practice' may appear to be a desirable combination of focus on both form and meaning. Such work generally involves getting learners to handle a set of samples representing a grammatical unit while ensuring that the handling of each sample involves some attention to its meaning. Both the samples of language and the meaning are made available (in more or less direct ways) and learners' attention alternates repeatedly between the two, it being a constraint of the activity that each be paid attention to. Such activity differs qualitatively from what we have called 'meaning-focused' activity in that the latter involves only attention to meaning as a constraint. While meaning-focused activity accepts the consequence that any abstraction of language structure will be unpredictable in its occurrence and varied in its results, 'meaningful practice' fails to bring about a sustained preoccupation with meaning, not only because of its constant shift of attention between meaning and form but, more importantly, because of the need for the different samples of language to be similar in grammatical structure in order for the activity to count as 'practice' at all. The notion of practice demands a paradigmatic occurrence of similarly structured samples, while a sustained preoccupation with meaning demands developing discourse which tends to operate syntagmatically through structurally dissimilar samples. Moreover, since meaningful practice involves a prediction by the teacher of the language forms to be employed by learners, it involves a prediction of meaning-content as well and, for that reason, finds it difficult to accommodate negotiable meaning-content or procedures by which learners derive – with varied and unpredictable success – new meaning-content from that which is given. As argued in the previous chapter, the processes by which learners derive meaning and make it their own are important for meaning-focused activity.

There is a further notion relating to pre-selection which involves ensuring the occurrence of samples representing a given grammatical unit by selecting classroom activities in which such samples are predictable. The idea is that the samples will then occur naturally in the classroom, thus providing the predicted exposure for learners, while at the same time allowing a sustained preoccupation with meaning. No planned repetition or practice is involved and only the teacher, not the learner, needs (it is thought) to be aware of the pre-selection. The question here is not only to what extent samples representing particular units of grammar are, in general, predictable in particular situations but also, and more important, what effect the teacher's act of making the prediction has on the resulting classroom discourse. If a prediction is made, it must matter whether or not it comes true, and the success of the prediction must therefore be, for the teacher, a part of the criterion of success for the activity concerned. As a result, there is at least a desire on the part of the teacher to see the prediction come true and, very likely, a consequent attempt to ensure that it does. This means that the teacher will try to scan his own language grammatically while he is employing it in discourse – an operation unnatural to language use and unlike deployment – or to 'plant' the predicted samples deliberately in the discourse, and perhaps highlight them as language forms in some way. The effect is that the teacher is not as meaning-focused as the learners and the resulting discourse as a whole is less meaning-focused than it would otherwise be. The only justification for such a sacrifice in the quality of discourse is planned progression, the value of which was questioned above.[9] If planned progression and a planned focus on form are both excluded, it then becomes immaterial which samples of language occur or recur in particular classroom activities, as long as some do. Language therefore becomes free to select itself according to the needs of the activity/discourse and manageability for learners, which is precisely the case with meaning-focused activity.

Language awareness

It is not claimed that meaning-focused activity eliminates all attention by learners to language samples as form. Such total elimination is probably impossible in any form of teaching, and possibly inconsistent with normal language use. The claim is rather that meaning-focused activity ensures that any attention to form is (1) contingent to dealing with meaning and (2) self-initiated (i.e. not planned, predicted, or controlled by the teacher). Such self-initiated attention to form may in fact have value for learning in that it is likely to be engendered either by the process of meaning-extraction/meaning-expression or by the internal process of structure-abstraction and, in either case, to have a facilitative role to play. Attention to form which is externally initiated or manipulated is likely to remain unrelated to either process and can only be a pedagogic objective in itself.

Learners in project classes were, of course, aware that it was English that was being used in the classroom and that they were being taught English in this way. They often asked to know the meaning or pronunciation of particular words, just as they asked for particular statements to be repeated or explained. They found themselves trying to guess, consciously, the meaning of particular expressions or to find some way of saying what they wished to say – perhaps by 'borrowing' available language. More significantly, there were indications that individual learners became suddenly preoccupied, for a moment, with some piece of language, in ways apparently unrelated to any immediate demands of the ongoing activity in the classroom. For example there was sometimes a repeated mouthing by the learner of a word or a longer stretch of language to himself, or a prolonged gaze at something that was written on the blackboard or on paper, or a retrospective alteration of, or deliberation on, something the learner himself had written earlier in a notebook. Very occasionally, there was an out-of-context request to the teacher or a fellow-learner to confirm, or just listen to, a reading or repetition of something that had been written or said. The result, in all cases, was a temporary withdrawal from the activity or interaction on hand, which was what made the phenomenon noticeable. It was not, however, a phenomenon which was noticed frequently or equally by different teachers, or equally in different classes, and it was only when a teacher had been teaching a class for some time and was used to the ways of particular learners that it began to be noticed at all. It is possible to speculate whether such moments of involuntary language awareness might be symptoms (or 'surfacings') of some internal process of learning, representing, for instance, a conflict in the emerging internal system leading to a system-revision. If so, one could further speculate whether the frequency of such symptoms might be an indicator of the pace of system-development and therefore a correlate of differential achievement between learners. (A 'fossilized' learner might then represent the case where 'conflict' and system-revision have ceased to occur.) It is, however, difficult to see what deliberate use could be made, in teaching, of such a perception: if the instances of involuntary awareness are symptoms of some learning process, any attempt to increase or influence them directly would be effort misdirected to symptoms, rather than to causes.

One might also try to relate the language awareness occasioned by system-development to other forms of language awareness occasioned by system-operation outside a learning context, in normal language use. There are, for instance, moments of language awareness which occur when one has lost track of a sentence half-way through or when one registers a linguistic deviance, the former representing a lapse in the internal system's operation, and the latter a mismatch or conflict between one's internal system and what is being processed. The latter is especially suggestive in that the linguistic deviance gets registered 'vaguely' while the sample of language concerned is being processed for its meaning – a phenomenon analogous to that hypothesized above as language learning, namely that of structure being abstracted subconsciously from a piece of language while the learner is consciously occupied with its meaning. A form of language awareness also occurs during discourse-planning when one tries out some expression or verbal formulation on oneself before speaking or writing it, or in the course of retrospectively checking what one has written when one tests a verbal formulation to see if it 'sounds right' grammatically.[10] There is also the language awareness which is referred to in linguistic analysis as the speaker's intuition, and treated as evidence on the linguistic competence being investigated. Some of these forms of awareness are noticeable in the classroom too: learners sometimes appear to be planning pieces of discourse – deliberating with a verbal formulation, even mouthing it before writing it down or making an intervention in oral interaction.

While on the subject of language awareness, it may be worthwhile mentioning one other phenomenon. Explicit grammar rules 'make sense' when they accord with language samples arising from or conforming to one's own competence, and there is often a sense of satisfaction or of discovery when that happens: what one has 'known' without being aware of it is now confirmed as being right (hence the satisfaction) and is also seen to be rule-governed (hence the sense of discovery). It is tempting to see this phenomenon as an argument for rule-focused activity or, within task-based teaching, for tasks involving rule-discovery, but it is important to remember that the sense of satisfaction arises only because the rule is authenticated by data originating in one's own competence – that is to say, when one has already developed an internal system capable of yielding samples which conform to the rule.[11] When that is not the case, rules are just so much complex information and the situation is not dissimilar to that of trying to read a grammar book of a language one does not know. Setting tasks of rule-discovery before learners have developed an adequate internal system will, correspondingly, be putting them in the situation of a 'structural linguist' attempting to construct the grammar of a language he does not know. Further, the sense of satisfaction and discovery does not imply that the explicit rule of grammar concerned is, in fact, the rule of the internal system. (If it did, we would not be witnessing different schools of linguistics proposing different rules and models of grammar, all with a sense of discovery and satisfaction.) All it implies is some pleasant surprise at output-similarity between the rule and the internal system. This similarity is generally on a very limited scale, in terms of both the amount of data involved and depth of awareness: generations of teachers and learners of English no doubt derived satisfaction for earlier analyses of 'John is eager/ easy to please', before transformational grammar came on the scene.

Comprehension and production

It was suggested above that comprehension and production are both of value to the development of the internal system in that they both bring about a deployment of available abstract structures and thereby a firming-up of those structures. It was also suggested that comprehension brings about the formation of new abstract structures as well as a revision or extension of existing ones, the latter as a result of some form of matching between the structures being deployed and those embodied in the sample of language being comprehended. Comprehension precedes production because abstract structures need to be formed relatively firmly before they are deployed in production. It is possible to point to four factors which help to explain the difference between deployment in comprehension and in production.

First, comprehension is a private activity, not perceptible to others. Production involves a display of language and therefore causes a sense of insecurity. One can afford to fumble, backtrack, or try out different possibilities in comprehension, without revealing one's incompetence or losing face, while any such strategies in production run the risk of being noticed. Learners therefore need a relatively high level of linguistic confidence (arising from a relatively firmly-formed internal system) to engage in production. There are, no doubt, other sources of confidence and insecurity arising from individual characteristics of learners which interact with linguistic confidence; the point being made here is simply that there is a particular form of linguistic confidence which derives from the firmness of the internal system and is demanded more in production than in comprehension.

Secondly, deployment in comprehension is a matter of the abstract structures of the internal system being mapped onto those which are already embodied in given language samples, while deployment in production is a matter of internal structures creating and supporting new language samples. It is easier for unstable or faintly-formed structures to be 'invoked' in comprehension than for them to be 'embodied' in production. Further, comprehension can be partial or selective – confined to as much of the language as is possible, or necessary for the purpose on hand – without there being any sense that the sample of language being comprehended is affected by such incomplete processing. Production, in comparison, calls for a fulness or completeness of linguistic formulation which is determined not just by the learner's ability and the strict needs of the meaning-exchange being attempted, but by the requirements of language structure as well. Learners, of course, produce linguistic formulations which are as full as their internal systems can support but there nevertheless seems to be some awareness that the formulations are less full than they need to be – and a sense of responsibility for that fact. It is possible that the teacher's incidental reformulation of learners' linguistic formulations contributes to this awareness but it is also likely that the awareness reflects the fact that the internal system is not fully realized in production, that unstable or faintly-formed structures are not being deployed. There is also the fact that incompleteness in learners' processing of a sample is not visible to the teacher while incompleteness in linguistic formulations stands out clearly, thus creating an exaggerated impression of the difference in learners' abilities in comprehension and production.

Thirdly, and relatedly to the above, the degree of commitment or precision in comprehension is controlled by the comprehender: it is possible to hold some choices between possible meanings 'in abeyance' and to operate without commitment to particular interpretations, leaving it to future occasions to make greater precision possible. Production, however, involves verbal explicitness and the words employed can commit the producer to unintended meaning-content. This, too, makes production more of a risk than comprehension and therefore dependent on a higher level of confidence.

Fourthly, comprehension can draw on extra-linguistic resources, such as knowledge of the world and contextual expectations, which can support linguistic resources to the extent necesssary and do not need to be marked off from them: the complementary relationship between linguistic resources and extra-linguistic ones, that is to say, is controlled by the comprehender and is readily adjustable. Production, by contrast, is much more language dependent and, when it is inadequate, has to depend on the listener/reader drawing on such extra-linguistic resources as are available: the producer, that is to say, cannot control the use of extra-linguistic resources by his audience. Any use of extra-linguistic resources by the producer himself is, moreover, marked off clearly from linguistic ones and can be seen as a public admission of linguistic inadequacy. Production thus involves a greater sense of dependence on linguistic resources than does comprehension.

Differences such as these help to explain why comprehension can take place from the beginning of language learning while production becomes feasible only at a much later stage. They also show that the best preparation for production is continual comprehension, since it is recurrent deployment in comprehension that can firm up the internal system to a point at which it becomes deployable in production. This is not to say that production itself has no value for further production: deployment in production, when it has become possible, also helps to firm up the internal system, thus making it more deployable in subsequent production. Since, however, initial readiness for production is not predictable, not observable and not likely to be uniform for different learners, all that pedagogy can do is to (1) ensure continual deployment in comprehension, (2) provide recurrent opportunity for production in case any learner is ready to attempt it at a given point, and (3) guard against the possibility that an inability to attempt production holds back deployment in comprehension. Task-based activity in the classroom involves comprehension at all stages and provides opportunity for production in the pre-task interaction with the teacher and in stating the outcomes of individual tasks, but also allows learners (deliberately, in the early stages) to use alternatives to production such as numbers, diagrams, or 'borrowed' language to the extent necessary for carrying out the activity.[12] What is excluded is 'reproduction' in the sense of planned repetition or externally-initiated borrowing (see pages 60–61), as being of little value in making production possible.

Groupwork

The project did not use groupwork in the classroom, in the sense of putting learners in small groups and asking or encouraging them to attempt tasks jointly. Learners were, however, given the right at the 'task' stage to consult fellow-learners or the teacher if they wished to, either briefly or to an extent amounting to collaboration. In practice, some learners made more use of this right than others and on some occasions more than on others. The avoidance of groupwork in a more organized form was, at the beginning of the project, due to a wish to confine pedagogic exploration to the project's major principle (i.e. the significance of meaning-focused activity in the classroom) which did not in itself entail groupwork; but more positive reasons for excluding it came to the perceived in the course of the project.

The strongest argument for systematic groupwork in task-based teaching would be that it will generate spontaneous interaction between members of a group, creating opportunities for the deployment of their emerging internal systems. But deployment, as noted above, is a process during which learners' internal systems get firmed up (in production as well as in comprehension) and revised or extended (in comprehension). Opportunity for revision or extension arises when there is a mismatch between the internal system being deployed and that embodied in the sample of language being processed – when, that is to say, the internal system encounters 'superior data' or, in other words, samples of language which embody a more highly developed internal system. It is important for learners' internal systems to be continually encountering 'superior data' so that the process of firming up is balanced by a process of revision and extension. Since differences between the internal systems of different learners are much smaller than those between the internal systems of the learners as a group and that of the teacher, sustained interaction between learners is likely to provide much less opportunity for system-revision. As a result, the effect of learner-learner interaction will largely be a firming-up of learners' systems: each learner's output will reinforce the internal systems of the others without there being a corresponding process of revision, or at least with less of a balance between firming up and revision than when the teacher is a party to the interaction. There will then be a risk of fossilization – that is to say of learners' internal systems becoming too firm too soon and much less open to revision when superior data are available. The principle that interaction between the teacher and the learner, or between a text/ task on paper and the learner, is more beneficial than interaction between one learner and another is thus part of the concept of learning which lies behind task-based teaching. It is true that the voluntary consultation or collaboration between learners which was allowed, and often took place, in the project classrooms is open to the same effects of learner-learner interaction, but there was at least no pressure from the teacher on learners either to engage in such interaction or to conduct the interaction in the target language. Undue pressure on speaking in the target language can also have the effect of firming up the internal system prematurely.

A second major argument for organized groupwork is that small peer-groups provide a mutually supportive environment for learners which is less threatening than interaction with the teacher. But at least some learners find it more humiliating to lose face in front of their peers than in front of the teacher: they wish to see themselves as being equal to the former, but not to the latter. Also, some learners wish to work alone, to prove to themselves that they can succeed in doing the task without help. Learners have contrasting personalities: some are gregarious, some individualistic, some dominating, some shy. There are also likes and dislikes, and patterns of rivalry, friendship, and aspiration in the context of the class as a social group. To expect learners to shed or subdue such feelings of conflict in the interests of better second language learning is idealistic, and to cast the teacher in a threatening role and see learners as mutually supportive individuals seems simplistic. What sometimes happens, when the teacher insists on groupwork, is that learners feel a sense of resentment against the teacher himself, thus complicating the existing mix of feelings and attitudes in the class. What is probably most supportive is for the teacher to give learners the right to seek or not to seek help from peers on any given occasion.

Groupwork is sometimes advocated on the grounds that it increases the amount of language practice which each learner gets, but it will have become clear from the discussion in this chapter that the notion of 'practice' (i.e. reproduction, whether or not it is disguised in some way to look like production) has little relevance to the concept of learning which informs task-based teaching. It is also argued that interaction between peers involves certain forms of language use or certain illocutionary functions which the 'unequal' interaction between teacher and learner does not bring into play, but the relevance of that argument is unclear for a pedagogic approach which (1) aims to develop learners' grammatical competence and (2) claims that the grammatical competence which develops through deployment will be deployable generally in different forms and functions of language use.

Notes

1 See for instance, Davies *et al.* (1984) for a comprehensive picture of current concerns in the study of acquisition.

2 Linguistic (or grammatical) competence in Chomsky's sense, i.e. 'the system of rules and principles that we assume have, in some manner, been internally represented by the person who knows a language and that enable the speaker, in principle, to understand an arbitrary sentence and to produce a sentence expressing his thought' (1980: 201).

3 What motivates the internal system to go beyond the strict needs of meaning-exchange remains a matter of speculation in first as much as in second language learning. See Brown (1973: 463–4) on first language learning: 'What impels the child to "improve" his speech at all remains something of a mystery.... It is surprisingly difficult to find cases in which omission (of requisite morphemes in a child's speech) resulted in incomprehension or misunderstanding.' It is, of course, easy to find instances of second language learning in which the internal system has apparently stopped short of full development but it is equally easy to find other instances, in which similar conditions obtain, where it has developed far more fully. Second language pedagogy can in fact be viewed as a matter of creating certain learning conditions in which the internal process of system development is likely to go 'further' than in other conditions.

4 See Chomsky (1976: 23) and Chomsky (1979: 82–4).

5 See Corder (1981: 65–78).

6 There is of course the poorly understood phenomenon of fossilization (see note 3 above).

7 See Corder (1981: 66).

8 I take Brumfit's (1984a: 56–9) argument for using accuracy and fluency activities separately (instead of attempting to integrate them operationally) to be a recognition of this conflict.

9 Another possible justification is coverage of language structure. This will be discussed in the next chapter.

10 Such phenomena can be regarded as a form of monitoring, but monitoring should then be seen as a deliberate tapping of language competence (i.e. of the 'acquired' system), in order to overcome the effect of performance factors (in Chomsky's sense of 'performance'), not as a scanning of the output with the help of a separate, consciously-learnt system of rules, as Krashen suggests. Such a tapping of competence is what happens when speakers of a language, who may never have 'learnt' any grammar rules, exercise their linguistic 'intuitions' (also in Chomsky's sense) to judge features such as well-formedness and ambiguity. It also operates in self-correction and in the production of planned discourse (as in careful – hence relatively slow – speech or writing). What Krashen regards as monitoring seems to me to be largely, if not entirely, a matter of competence tapping, and I therefore do not see any case for teaching descriptive grammar to learners 'for monitor use' (1982: 76–8). Notice also that teaching grammar for monitor use implies an assumption of isomorphism between the descriptive grammar to be taught and the learner's internal system.

11 One recalls that Palmer (1917) suggested that formal grammar should follow the learning of a language, not precede it. See also Brumfit's (1984a: 40) quotation of Locke's statement in 1693: 'If grammar is taught at any time, it must be to one who can speak the language already.' The fact that many adult second language learners ask to be taught grammar may be partly due to some earlier experience of satisfaction from post-acquisition grammar. Such experience may also explain why many successful second language learners make 'introspective'

statements about grammar having been useful or even essential for them in learning the language concerned (see Pickett 1978). It is not at all surprising that attempts to introspect on language learning should result in a recall and highlighting of what was most memorable from that experience.

12 This is not to say that it is always possible for the teacher to know when a learner is producing, and when he or she is borrowing language; nor is it necessary, in teaching, to be able to tell the one from the other. It is conceivable that borrowing has some direct value for the development of the internal system – that the matching of one's own meaning with a piece of language one has identified or selected brings about some 'intensive exposure' to that piece of language, in the way purposeful comprehension does.

5   Syllabus and Materials

This chapter discusses some implications of task-based teaching for syllabuses and materials in second language pedagogy. It will be argued that task-based teaching calls not only for different syllabuses and materials from those used in other forms of teaching but for a modification of the concepts of syllabus and materials as well.

A syllabus is generally thought of as a statement of what is to be taught. But the expression 'what is to be taught' may refer either to what is to be done in the classroom or what is to be learnt as a result. This discussion will refer to what is to be done as an 'operational construct' and what is to be learnt as an 'illuminative construct'. There are also other roles which are often assigned to a syllabus and comment will be made on two of them; the syllabus as an instrument of organizational control, and the syllabus as a document of public consent.[1]

Syllabus as an operational construct

The syllabus is a form of support to the teaching activity that is to be carried out in the classroom and a form of guidance in the construction of appropriate lesson plans. It is concerned, from this point of view, with what is to be done in the classroom, not necessarily with what is perceived to be taught or learnt thereby; its role is essentially to make it possible for one teacher to draw on the experience of another – for many teachers to draw on the experience of some. A syllabus in this role was an immediate need for the teaching done on the project: those who taught early project classes made their experience available (in the form of a collection of tasks which they had found feasible and satisfying, in the sequence in which they had used them) to those who taught later classes at comparable levels of ability. This transmission of lesson plans from one teacher to another was in a very specific form, and the only step taken towards generalization was a descriptive or mnemonic labelling of different tasks and a listing of them in an order suggested both by experience and some reflection on it.[2] The list was called a 'procedural syllabus', with the intention of indicating that it was only a specification of what might be done in the classroom – that is to say, only an operational construct. The tasks in the collection were set out in a 'pre-task and task' format with, in addition, an indication of the success achieved by the class which had first attempted the task: this indication in itself was a form of procedural guidance.[3] The teachers who drew on the collection in the teaching of later project classes altered the sequencing of tasks at various points, modified the content of some of the tasks in order to raise or lower the difficulty level as well as to 'localize' information where necessary, and omitted or added tasks within given task-sequences. This was done for the purpose of maintaining the more general principle of reasonable challenge for each class at each stage of teaching; so the principle of reasonable challenge itself can be regarded as a further, more general, form of procedural guidance.

The low level of generality represented by a list of actual tasks was adequate for the scale of teaching attempted on the project, but task-based teaching on a larger scale would naturally call for a more generalized construct capable of supporting activity in more varied classrooms. This could be attempted by stating task-types, instead of specific tasks, indicating the types of information to be used (rules, schedules, prices, distances); the forms of demand to be made on the learner (inference, calculation, collation of information, application of rules to particular cases), and the types of constraint to be observed (the shortest time or distance, the lowest cost, the most symmetrical pattern). The list given in Appendix V represents one possible level of generality in task specification.

It is also possible to indicate some criteria for grading tasks, as rough measures of cognitive complexity. Experience on the project suggests the following parameters:

1 *Information provided* The amount of information to be handled makes a task more or less difficult; so does variety in the types or sources of information. Tasks based on rules become more difficult when there is an increase in the number of rules; they also become more difficult when there are rules of different kinds, or when the personal circumstances of the rule-user have to be borne in mind as well.

2 *Reasoning needed* The 'distance' between the information provided and the information to be arrived at as outcome – i.e. the number of steps involved in the deduction, inference, or calculation – is a measure of the relative difficulty of tasks. Working out a teacher's personal timetable from given class timetables is easier

than working out, from the same information, the time when two teachers are both free.

3 *Precision needed* The same information may need to be interpreted more or less precisely for different tasks, and outcomes may need to be expressed in more or less precise terms as well. Difficulty-level increases with the degree of precision called for. Instructions to draw demand more and more precision in processing as they are aimed at more and more complex figures as outcomes. Precision is partly a matter of the number of plausible options: the larger the range of plausible options, the more difficult it is to decide on the one which represents the right outcome. It also has a dimension of linguistic accuracy: precise interpretation is often a matter of accurate comprehension of language, and precision in stating outcomes can depend on lexical or syntactic accuracy.

4 *Familiarity with constraints* Learners' knowledge of the world can make tasks more or less difficult for them, depending on whether they are more or less familiar with purposes and constraints of the kind involved in the tasks. Tasks based on money earned and money spent proved easier for project classes than those based on a bank account (though deposits and withdrawals from an account might be said to have the same role as income and expenditure). Students found tasks based on the baggage rules of air travel difficult because the distinction between check-in baggage and hand baggage was too unfamiliar a concept.

5 *Degree of abstractness* Working with concepts is more difficult than working with the names of objects or actions. With tasks based on information about books, students found it difficult to handle the category of publishing, as distinct from that of writing, printing, or selling books. Categorization of kinship according to generation (for example an uncle represents an earlier generation than a brother, whether or not he is actually older than the brother) was a task-type that proved to be too difficult for a project class.

The fact that tasks which occurred early in a new sequence tended to use only information-gaps while subsequent tasks were based on reasoning-gaps was mentioned in Chapter 3 and can be viewed as a special case of grading by the reasoning required. It was also mentioned (in Chapter 2) that a change from orally presented tasks to similar ones presented in writing proved to provide a distinct increase in difficulty for project classes – perhaps because writing, which represents language at one remove, adds to the 'distance' between language samples and meaning content. Similarly, there was a gradual increase in the amount and complexity of the language used in presenting tasks, with a consequent decrease in reliance on non-linguistic modes for presenting information. This can itself be regarded as a dimension of grading, although it was purely in response to learners' increasing abilities.

While generality in specification can be attempted in ways such as the above, it is important to bear in mind that the purpose of generalizing is to help 'translate' an operational construct from one teaching situation to another, not to arrive at some fixed specification which removes the need for teachers' choices and decisions. No syllabus of generalized tasks can identify or anticipate all the sources of challenge to particular learners, and what constitutes reasonable challenge for a given class depends, in any case, on such factors as the learners' knowledge of the world and cognitive state, the teacher's ability to give help through simplification or negotiation, and his or her assessment of learners' success. A procedural syllabus cannot therefore be judged by its generality or specificity as such.[4] As an operational construct, it can only be assessed by its operability – i.e. whether it provides the degree of support which is thought, or found by trial and error, to be necessary for some of the teacher's decisions, without pre-empting other decisions which the teacher needs to make independently.

Syllabus as an illuminative construct

While the syllabus as an operational construct is concerned with procedures of teaching, the syllabus as an illuminative construct is concerned with the product of learning: it is a specification of what is to be learnt in terms of a conceptual model which aims to provide an understanding (hence the term 'illuminative') of the nature of the subject area concerned. Descriptive grammars are attempts to provide an understanding of the structure of language, the different 'schools' of grammar employing different conceptual models for the purpose; and a grammatical syllabus is, from the point of view of task-based teaching, an illuminative construct. A 'content' syllabus may be said to be an illuminative construct which is also used as an operational construct, while a procedural syllabus is an operational construct which is deliberately different from illuminative constructs. A content syllabus is appropriate when the aim of teaching is an understanding by learners of the subject concerned, or when the development of an ability in learners is thought to be directly controllable in terms of the relevant illuminative construct. A procedural syllabus is justified when the ability to be developed is perceived as a matter of natural 'organic' growth and teaching is directed to creating conditions which are most favourable to that process.[5] To take examples from other fields of activity, farming operations can be regarded as a procedural syllabus; so can procedures of physical training, and play-school activities meant to help infants' conceptual or perceptual development.

The use of a procedural syllabus for language teaching is not a denial of any role to illuminative constructs in language pedagogy, much less a questioning of the value or validity of illuminative constructs as conceptual models. The perception of language development as organic growth is itself a conceptual model, and pedagogic perceptions can be articulated and discussed only in terms of whatever illuminative constructs are relevant. The arguments stated in earlier chapters about the probable complexity of the internal system which represents grammatical competence, the development of that system as a holistic process, and the formation, deployment, and revision of abstract cognitive structures, have all drawn on illuminative constructs for their articulation. Similarly, any attempt to validate pedagogy by examining learning outcomes also needs to draw on some illuminative construct of the product of learning. If teaching aims to develop in learners an ability to conform subconsciously to grammatical norms while the conscious mind is occupied with meaning exchange, an illuminative construct of those grammatical norms (i.e. a descriptive grammar) needs to be drawn on in examining the degrees of conformity achieved by learners under conditions of preoccupation with meaning-exchange. The syllabus as an illuminative construct thus has roles in pedagogy which are different from that of an operational construct but are relevant in justifying the use of a particular operational construct. What seems unreasonable is any assumption that a syllabus as an operational construct must necessarily be an illuminative construct – or that any operational construct used as a syllabus must meet the same criteria as are applicable to illuminative constructs.[6]

Syllabus as an instrument of organizational control

The syllabus is also a means by which supervisory control is exercised in institutionalized education and a basis on which common examinations are set for learners in different classrooms. Supervisory control can consist of some form of monitoring of classrooms to ensure that the activities that take place are those that are meant to, and a comparison of progress in different classrooms. I will be commenting in the next chapter on the expectation of uniformity in teaching which supervision often implies, but I do not see any serious conflict between the use of a procedural syllabus and the need for supervisory control as such: it is as easy or difficult to monitor task-based activity in classrooms as it is to monitor language-practice activity. The complexity of the tasks which learners in different classrooms are able to perform at any given time, and with a given degree of success, seems to me a usable basis of comparison – less objective, perhaps, than a comparison based on an itemized linguistic syllabus but, I would argue, likely to be more valid as an indication of true learning. Common examinations, too, can be set in the form of tasks and, since tasks have an essential similarity to real-life language use in their preoccupation with meaning-content, success in such examinations can be expected to correlate acceptably with success in real-life language use.

Syllabus as a document of public consent

Yet another role attributed to syllabuses is that of making educational intentions available for public criticism and of thereby acting as documents of public consent. One can readily agree that the overall aims of teaching should be open to scrutiny and consent by the society in which that teaching (and learning) takes place, but this does not mean that a syllabus for public discussion should necessarily be either an illuminative construct or an operational one. The aim of task-based teaching – to enable the learner to acquire an ability to employ language for meaning exchange and, in the process, to achieve conformity to linguistic norms – does not seem to me to be at variance with the general view of what language ability is. What pedagogic means are best employed to realize an agreed aim, for example whether the operational construct should be a content syllabus or a procedural one, is an educational decision rather than a social one. There is, of course, a form of conditioning of the public mind which results from past practice in education (for example the view that teaching a language 'properly' is teaching its grammar) but that is something which any pedagogic innovation has to come to terms with. There have, after all, been changes in the mode of syllabus specification in the past and it is difficult to see how the role of a syllabus as a public document in itself constitutes a strong argument against a procedural syllabus.

Simple and sophisticated syllabuses

Since a procedural syllabus aims only to support classroom activity, it needs only to be as general or specific (and as structured or unstructured) as is necessary for that purpose. A content syllabus, by contrast, lends itself to much greater internal structuring, drawing for the purpose on one or more illuminative constructs, and can look much more 'impressive' than a procedural syllabus. There is also, I think, a general notion that highly-structured syllabuses, being 'rich' in detail, are indicators of superior forms of pedagogy. One result of the communicative teaching movement in recent years, for instance, has been the construction of multi-dimensional syllabuses, making simultaneous use of two or more illuminative constructs of language or language use which include those in terms of notions, functions, settings, topics, register and discourse, as well as grammar and lexis. Specific attention to a variety of dimensions tends to be viewed as an expression of educational responsibility, while simultaneous systematicity in terms of different dimensions makes the syllabus look 'rich' – or systematically complex – suggesting that the resulting teaching and learning are correspondingly effective or efficient. In reality, however, such complexity in syllabus design can have the general effect of reducing the range of language that can be used in teaching materials or the classroom. Each dimension to a syllabus is a criterion for the choice of language samples to be used – that is to say, for the delimitation of language. If a sample of language has to meet two criteria simultaneously, it has fewer alternatives available than if it has to meet only one criterion. Samples of language which can fit five or six predetermined categories simultaneously (for example expound a function, be appropriate to a setting, be relevant to a topic, exemplify a point of grammar, and be natural to a given form of discourse or a given participant-relationship) can be so specific that teaching is reduced to focusing on a fixed list of language forms. Much teaching based on such syllabuses no doubt stops short of this level of restriction, but it is important to bear in mind that the process of enriching syllabus-design can also be one of impoverishing classroom language and that the more 'content' a syllabus has in the sense of 'detail', the less exposure to language the learner is likely to get.

Syllabuses organized in terms of 'communicative' content (for example functions and topics) can also claim to have the additional advantage of being divisible into stages such that each stage represents a distinct level of learner achievement, and has an immediate surrender value.[7] In contrast, a procedural syllabus of tasks only envisages constant effort by learners to deploy their language resources in the classroom, and does not attempt either to demarcate areas of real-life use for different stages of teaching or to bring about a 'thorough' learning of use in some functions at each stage. While this can be regarded as a reflection of the fact that the teaching that was done on the project was free from social demands for immediate usefulness there is, I think, a more general point to make about immediate usefulness and the quality of learning. Syllabuses can be set up either as a sequence of fixed levels of expected achievement or as a general direction for learners' progress. A fixed-level syllabus implies a demand that all learners reach a common level of achievement at a certain stage and therefore the assumption that learning depends relatively directly on teaching. A syllabus seen as a general direction of progress, on the other hand, implies the recognition that learning depends necessarily on the learner (i.e. on what he or she brings to bear on the process) and that progress will necessarily vary between different learners. Although it would be simplistic to suggest that learners' actual progress is influenced by whether the syllabus is perceived one way or the other by the teacher, it is, I think, possible to suggest that the teacher's perception of the syllabus has an influence on the form of teaching employed and on the quality of learning achieved. When a syllabus is seen in fixed-level terms, there is likely to be a preference for forms of teaching which can bring about relatively uniform levels of learning.[8] Since forms of learning which depend directly on teaching – and can be seen to be both thorough and uniform – are set patterns of behaviour, teaching is likely to take the form of training in fixed patterns of verbal behaviour, at some cost to the longer-term development of capacity for adaptable behaviour and potential for further learning.[9] The more frequent the fixed stages are in a syllabus (thus increasing the immediacy of surrender values), the more behaviour-oriented the teaching and learning are likely to be. This can only result in a gradual reduction of the notion of language to a matter of meeting

short-term needs, and the activity of language teaching to a matter
of equipping learners quickly with linguistic table-manners.

Materials

Any collection of tasks acting as materials for task-based teaching
can only have the status of source books for teachers, not of course
books. Although it is possible to organize the collection in some
order of increasing task-complexity (with tasks of the same type
appearing in short sequences, at various points, and with later task-
types exploiting the kinds of reasoning, content-familiarity, or
format-familiarity likely to result from earlier ones), the ordering
has necessarily to be partial and suggestive rather than definitive,
because what constitutes reasonable challenge for any class at any
time is unpredictable and depends, as noted already, both on the
learners' ability and on the degree of help given by the teacher.[10]
Teachers should therefore be free to modify the information-
content or reasoning-gap of some tasks, omit some tasks or alter
their sequence and, when possible, devise their own tasks and add
them to the collection.

The language in which tasks are presented in a collection is
similarly subject to teachers' simplification in the classroom,
including, when necessary, a complete reformulation. Although the
same task can, within limits, be presented and attempted in more or
less complex language, there is, in general, a minimal level of
linguistic ability which a given task demands of the learner, and
different teachers may assess that minimal level differently,
depending on the degree of simplification they consider feasible and
on their earlier experience of trial and error. Teachers' decisions
about what task to use at what time thus involve an assessment of
both cognitive complexity and linguistic feasibility, the aim being to
ensure that the tasks used are, in both respects, difficult but
manageable for learners.

The fact that materials need to be used as sources rather than as
pre-constructed courses should not be regarded as a weakness of
task-based teaching; it can in fact be a strength for any form of
teaching. When what is done in the classroom involves a decision
made by the teacher, he or she has an 'investment' in that activity
and consequently a reason to feel personally satisfied or dissatisfied
with the way in which it takes place. There is also a likelihood that
the outcome of each of the teacher's decisions will influence the

next one, and decision-making as such will improve from an accumulation of experience. Teaching is thus unlikely to become a matter of mere routine (see the discussion in the next chapter) and likely, instead, to contribute to the teacher's professional growth.[11] From this point of view, 'loosely constructed' teaching materials have the advantage not only of being more easily adaptable to particular classrooms but of promoting teachers' professional development over time. It is common to regard materials which are 'tightly constructed' (or fully specified) as being commendable on the grounds that they make teachers' work easy and ensure a uniformity to the work that takes place in different classrooms, in spite of differences between teachers. Indeed, it is often thought that materials are where pedagogic intentions are carried out in action, and where theory and practice are ingeniously fused: this is especially the case if the theory involves conflicting principles such as linguistic systematicity and natural samples of language, or planned language practice and learners' attention on meaning-content. The result is that pedagogic proposals tend to be assessed by how impressive and interesting to the observer – or interesting to the learner in the opinion of the observer – the associated materials look. While there is certainly a case for providing support to the teacher in the form of materials, there is also a need to be aware that materials which are, or are made out to be, superior to what teachers can hope to do on their own, restrict the teacher to the role of a transmitter of given materials to the learner, and a carrier out of instructions given to him by the materials. This means that the teacher's responsibility is to the materials rather than to learners, and the general effect of such non-negotiable materials is to reduce the degree of teachers' identification with what takes place in the classroom and therefore to reduce the likelihood of teachers' growth from the experience of teaching.

In task-based teaching, lessons in the classroom are not acts of text, or language presentation, but rather contexts for discourse creation.[12] The tasks provided in a collection are essentially plans for discourse, and the discourse which actually results in the classroom is shaped as much by learners' reactions as by teachers' intentions, and also by a number of *ad hoc* coping strategies employed on both sides. 'Materials', in the sense of the language that becomes available to learners, are the actual discourse events that constitute lessons.[13] Further, since those discourse events are likely to be perceived and processed differently by different learners, depending on the degree of their engagement and what they bring to bear on the tasks, materials as learning resources can vary from one learner to another within the same class.

Coverage

This perception of 'materials' makes it virtually impossible to monitor the occurrence of different items of language (structural or lexical units) in the classroom for the purpose of checking that specific areas of language structure have been covered. To ascertain the extent of linguistic coverage, it would be necessary to record and scan all the discourse that took place in a classroom over a period of time and, even then, the outcome of such scanning in one classroom would not be valid for another. Since no part of language structure can be learnt unless at least one instance of it becomes available to learners – since, that is to say, there can be no acquisition without exposure – the difficulty in ensuring coverage may appear to be a serious disadvantage. There may, in particular, appear to be a possibility that task-based teaching leads to the recurrence of the same, small set of language items over a long stretch of time and that learners, as a result, end up with highly restricted internal systems. It is therefore necessary to examine the notion of coverage and the risk in task-based teaching of leaving learners deprived of language data.

Even if we ignore, for the moment, the assumption of a correspondence between units of teaching and units of learning – an assumption commonly made in discussions of coverage – we still have to recognize that no form of teaching can possibly aim to teach 'all' of the units of language structure. A structural syllabus is necessarily a selection of linguistic units, made with the aim of enabling learners to learn *enough* of language structure in the classroom to be able to learn more, later and elsewhere, when more is encountered or needed. The notion of coverage is thus dependent on what is judged to form an adequate base for further learning. But it is difficult to identify a criterion for what constitutes this adequate base. Besides, any perception of the learner developing such a base has to take into account learning quality (what learning needs to be like in order to support further learning) and learning capacity (how much can be learnt, in a given time, without a sacrifice of quality). In the context of these latter notions, the question to ask is not what is likely to constitute adequate coverage in teaching, but rather (1) whether there is likely to be enough new language available, at every point, to cater for learning capacity, (2) whether what is learnt is likely to be the maximum possible for each learner, and (3) whether what is learnt is likely to be maximally supportive of further learning. The principle of reasonable challenge in task-based teaching aims to ensure that tasks in the classroom become steadily more complex at a pace determined by the learners' ability to cope, and there is, as noted earlier, a general increase in linguistic complexity as task complexity increases. Further, the fact that language-control by the teacher is not predetermined by any syllabus but responsive to actual need in the classroom, ensures that the limitation and simplification of language are at a level close to the minimum needed for learners to be able to manage. Since learners can manage with only a partial processing of the language being used in the classroom, there is likely to be more language available, on any occasion, than any learner is actually making use of. There is also the fact that the phenomenon referred to in Chapter 3 as 'task fatigue' creates a need for a regular change of task-types in the classroom. Finally, any language learnt in the classroom is learnt not as a result of any specific teaching of it, but as an incidental result of coping with meaning-exchange. This ensures that the learner has experience of coping with new language, and in the process learning it, in response to the needs of meaning-exchange – and is likely to be able to do the same outside the classroom. If, alternatively, what needs to be covered in teaching is thought of as being in some sense the 'core' of language structure, it might be asked how different the language represented by this 'core' is likely to be from that which occurs in the context of varied tasks in the classroom over a comparable period of time.

Teaching aids

The teaching aids used on the project were those which are used in most schools in India – namely, blackboard and chalk, and paper and pencil. Task-based teaching in other situations might draw upon such teaching aids as are easily available. The classroom in India is admittedly an austere one, but it is misleading to think of the quality of language pedagogy as being dependent on either the range of the teaching aids used or the technological sophistication of those aids. If, as has been argued, the essential condition for language learning is effort at meaning-exchange between language knowers and language learners, it is not of much importance what the meaning-exchange is about or what particular non-linguistic resources it is supported by. The possibilities of meaning-exchange cannot be said to be fewer in one society than in another and classrooms draw on those possibilities guided by practical considerations. Having to use only a blackboard and chalk is not, therefore, an 'impoverishment' of pedagogy in the sense of its being a sacrifice in effective learning. It is, further, important to avoid any assumption of a relationship between superior technology and superior pedagogy. There is no reason to expect any correlation between economic or technological development and either the quality of language use or success in language acquisition. Technology in the classroom can no doubt save labour for the teacher and perhaps also for the learner, but the labour so saved cannot be the labour of learning, and labour-saving does not necessarily create additional 'space' for learning. Technology in the classroom can also be a means of avoiding human error or limitation. However human error and inefficiency are among the causes of interaction and can therefore contribute to learning opportunity. There is also the risk that the use in the classroom of forms of technology which are unrelated to those in the society outside will give rise to pedagogic superstitions about the role of technological devices, and will leave teachers and learners trying to 'live up' to the machines being used.

Teachers' competence

The fact that English is taught in India – as in several other parts of the world – by non-native speakers of the language may seem to be a disadvantage for task-based teaching, since the teachers' own linguistic competence is, in general, limited or deficient in relation to native speaker's competence, and learners' acquisition will consequently be based on samples of language which are deviant in some respects. Some of the issues involved here have to do with the recruitment and training of teachers, but I will confine comment to two questions: (1) whether, in cases where the teacher's competence is limited, learners are likely to learn less from task-based teaching than from some other approach, and (2) whether the concept of deficiency in relation to native speakers' competence is a reasonable one to operate with anyway, given that English is an international language.

If a form of language pedagogy is to prevent learning from being influenced by the teacher's linguistic competence, it must of necessity chiefly comprise presenting predetermined samples of language to the learner. Any interaction or negotiation, involving spontaneous use of the language by the teacher, must be regarded as a hazard rather than a help in promoting the desired learning. Since, however, no lesson can be conducted without some verbal exchange between the teacher and the learner, this form of pedagogy must attempt to predict and pre-script classroom exchange in some way, giving priority to the more predeterminable forms of classroom exchange such as repetition by learners. It must also predict the learner's readiness to benefit from particular samples of language at particular times and attempt to ensure comprehensibility to the samples in advance of actual evidence from the learner. To the extent that such 'remote control' of classroom activity is feasible and successful, the learner is provided with desirable language samples but, at the same time, deprived of the condition in which he or she can benefit from them – the condition of deployment. To the extent the remote control does not, in fact, operate and the teacher is using language responsively and therefore spontaneously, better conditions are being provided for learning, albeit with samples of a lower quality. Since the quality of language samples is of consequence only insofar as the learner learns from them, it is reasonable – given the perception that learning takes place through deployment – to regard the benefit resulting from the teacher's spontaneous use of language as being greater than the loss resulting from the lower quality of samples. Given comparable learning conditions, however, it is equally reasonable to regard the *quality* of samples as being more important than their *quantity* – hence the avoidance of groupwork, as discussed in the previous chapter.

There is a further fact to bear in mind as well: trying to 'protect' the learner from any limitations or deficiencies in the teacher's language is also a process of undermining the teacher's professional self-confidence, and there is a danger of this causing a further loss both in the quality of what language the teacher uses spontaneously and the probability of responsive interaction with learners. Pedagogy has more to gain by seeking to benefit from what competence teachers have than by trying to safeguard against teachers' incompetence.

Turning now to the question of native-speaker standards, the fact that English is taught by large numbers of non-native speakers of the language in many parts of the world reflects its status as a world language, and it is necessary at some point to recognise that standards of adequacy for a world language are those which arise from its operation as such, not those which arise from its operation in exclusively native-speaking contexts. Besides, given the fact that most learners of English as a second language can only be taught by non-native speakers, a continuing assumption that native-speaker standards constitute measures of adequacy can only result in a sense of inadequacy in all the classrooms concerned. This assumption can also lead to a preference for forms of pedagogy which attempt a 'remote control' of second language classrooms and fail to accommodate developing perceptions of the nature of language learning.

Notes

1 See, for instance, Brumfit (1984c).

2 The 'procedural syllabus' included in the RIE Newsletter 1:4 (April, 1980) represents such an attempt, made at the end of the first year of the project.

3 Notice that the term 'procedural syllabus' is used in at least two senses: (1) a specification of classroom activities (including their meaning-content) which are, according to the theory behind task-based teaching, the procedures which bring about language learning, and (2) a specification of the patterns (or procedures) of classroom activity, but without any implications with respect to either language-content or meaning-content. A list of tasks or task-types is procedural in the first sense, while a specification of the 'pre-task and task' pattern is procedural in the second. Allwright (1976) uses the term 'procedural syllabus' in the second sense. Brumfit's (1984a:60–68) proposal for accuracy and fluency activities in the classroom can be said to be 'procedural' in the second sense, as can the listening-speaking-reading-writing cycle of S-O-S pedagogy.

4 Syllabuses in terms of language structure also vary between specificity (represented by 'citation' forms) and generality (represented by a metalinguistic specification of items). It is perhaps true to say, in general, that early structural syllabuses were marked by specificity (aiming to serve an operational purpose) while later ones attempted generality (drawing on the abstractions of structural linguistics and aiming to be illuminative).

5 The distinction commonly made between 'syllabus' and 'methodology' is generally the distinction between learning content and learning conditions. Thus, the methodological principles in S-O-S pedagogy of contextualization and controlled practice

indicate the conditions in which the items of a structural syllabus are thought to be learnt. Further, these conditions derive from perceived features of natural language use, for example automaticity, just as the condition aimed at in task-based teaching (a preoccupation with meaning) does.

6 See Brumfit (1984b:240): 'If the programme [i.e. the project in India] is shown to be successful and if a consistent pattern of cognitive procedures is reflected in the final ordering of materials, we may have the beginnings of an analysis of cognitive strategies in the acquisition of language.' What Brumfit envisages is the development of an illuminative construct from an operational one. I am unable to assess the feasibility of such a development but feel concerned about the effect on pedagogy of a 'final ordering of materials'. The fact that applied linguistics is an exploration of illuminative constructs does not imply that pedagogy invariably benefits from using illuminative constructs as operational ones.

   I am equally unable to see the force of Brumfit's argument for grammatical systematicity in the syllabus as an operational construct (1984a:98): 'The arguments in favour of systematicity are compelling. Whatever else we may not know about learning, we do know that what can be made systematic by the learner is more likely to be learnt than random elements, so – even if the system arrived at in describing language is not in fact the system that learners operate with – we should not discard, without strong reason, what can be made systematic for what cannot.' When 'the system that learners operate with' is seen to be different from 'the system arrived at in describing language', there seems to me to be no greater reason to use grammar to prevent randomness than to use the semantic structuring of tasks.

7 See Wilkins (1976:69–70). Michael West used the concept, as well as the term 'surrender value', in 1927, as Howatt (1984:245) points out.

8 It is, from this point of view, a 'hazard' of content syllabuses that they tend to be interpreted in fixed-level terms; and this points to a possible disadvantage of attempting to teach a second language by teaching one or more school subjects in it (as in 'immersion programmes'; see Swain and Lapkin 1982). Although such teaching will have the advantage of content-

systematicity, it will also have a commitment to a fixed body of content over a fixed time, which will reduce the adaptability of both content and pace to suit particular classes.

9 See Widdowson's (1983:6) distinction between 'training' and 'education'.

10 Allen and Widdowson (1974) represents an attempt to anticipate learners' need for help in reasoning and to provide for it in advance in the materials (see the sections entitled 'Solution' in different units). I think it illustrates both the advantage and the disadvantage of providing tasks in the form of a 'coursebook'.

11 It is interesting to speculate about the difference, in this respect, between those professions (for example medical and legal practice) in which each instance of professional work involves a fresh exercise of discretion and decision, and occupations (for example accounting, typing) in which routinization is much higher. Experience can lead either to improved judgement or firmly-formed routines and the balance between the two can be different in different fields of activity.

12 This is not, of course, to say that texts (i.e. pieces of writing) have no place in task-based teaching. Not only is the information relevant to a task regularly presented to learners on paper but the interpretation of reading texts can itself be designed as a problem-solving activity with questions involving inferencing or pattern-perception. The task cited in Brumfit (1984b) represents an early attempt (1981) to do this on the project.

13 See Allwright (1981) for a more forcefully stated case against the notion of 'coursebooks'.

6 Pedagogic Change

This short chapter is a statement of my view of the role of the project – and of pedagogic innovation generally – in educational change. As was pointed out in Chapter 1, the project was not an attempt to prove a teaching method through controlled experimentation. Equally, it should not be looked on as a field trial or pilot study leading to a large-scale statutory implementation. I think, indeed, that the value of statutory implementation as a means of bringing about better learning in a large number of classrooms is questionable generally, not so much because no single method can be suitable to varied teaching conditions or that teachers in any educational system are varied in their abilities, but much more because the quality of teaching in any classroom is dependent on the teacher's pedagogic perception, quite apart from his or her abilities and the teaching conditions.

Sense of plausibility

What a teacher does in the classroom is not solely, or even primarily, determined by the teaching method he or she intends to follow. There is a complex of other forces at play, in varied forms and degrees. There is often a desire to conform to prevalent patterns of teacher behaviour, if only for the sense of security such conformity provides. There is also a sense of loyalty to the past – both to the pattern of teaching which the teacher experienced when he or she was a student and to the pattern of his or her own teaching in the past. (Change in behaviour is a form of denial of the validity of past behaviour.) There is the teacher's self-image and a need to maintain status in relation to colleagues or the authorities. Above all, there is a relationship to maintain with a class of learners, involving factors such as interpretations of attitudes and feelings, anxieties about maintaining status or popularity, and fears about loss of face. A teacher's relationship with his or her class is based on constant and continuing contact; it therefore needs stability and finds change unsettling. Stability is provided by classroom routines which support shared expectations of behaviour and act as a framework for some balance between conflicting motives and self-images. Patterns of classroom activity, therefore, are not just teaching and learning procedures; more importantly, they are forms of routine through which teachers and learners play their appointed roles and regulate their relationship with one another.

One further factor in the teacher's 'mental mix' is a perception of how classroom activity leads to the desired outcome of learning. The nature of this perception varies between different teachers; some may see it as direct knowledge-transfer and others as a process mediated in some way. The degree of different teachers' awareness of it and their ability to articulate it may also vary. The perception may not be coherent or consistent and, in many cases, not deliberately developed or adopted. All teachers have been students in the past and draw, especially at the beginning of their teaching careers, on their memory of what *their* teachers did in the classroom and some interpretation of why. Initial teacher-training also provides procedures to serve as routines and some rationale for those procedures. These 'borrowed' perceptions acquire, in due course and in the process of actual continual teaching, what may be called a 'sense of plausibility' in the teacher's mind as he or she comes to identify with one or another of them. This identification need not always be with one of the perceptions 'borrowed' at the beginning; it can be with some amalgam of different perceptions, or with some new interpretation of one or more of them which has developed over time in the course of actual teaching. A teacher's 'intuition' can perhaps be said to be the perception which he or she identifies with (or feels a sense of plausibility about) in an unarticulated state.

Given this view, it is possible to think of the teacher's sense of plausibility as being engaged in some teaching activities but not in others. Both cases are examples of routines, but the complex of psychological factors held together by the routine differs in each. Where the teacher's sense of plausibility is not engaged, teaching is mere routine, which can only get more and more 'set' over time. However, this is not the case where there is some engagement of the teacher's sense of plausibility, for there is an 'investment' by the teacher in each lesson and a basis for feeling satisfied or dissatisfied with it. The teacher's sense of plausibility is then likely to be influenced in some way – strengthened, weakened, modified, extended, or brought into greater awareness – by the experience of teaching, and this, in turn, is likely to be an input to professional growth. There is thus an internal dynamic to teachers' daily work consisting of a more or less stable balance between different forces.

Impact of innovations

A new perception in pedagogy, implying a different pattern of classroom activity, is an intruder into teachers' mental frames – an unsettling one, because there is a conflict or mismatch between old and new perceptions and, more seriously, a threat to prevailing routines and to the sense of security dependent on them. If, however, there is no compulsion to adopt new routines (i.e. no statutory implementation), the sense of security is largely protected and teachers' existing perceptions may then begin to interact with the new one and to be influenced by it. The nature and extent of this influence will depend on what perceptions teachers are already operating with, how strong their sense of plausibility is about them, how firm or 'fluid' the mental frames are at the time, and so on. It will also depend on how powerful, well-articulated, or accessible the new perception is – how far, that is to say, it is able to invoke some corroborative experience in teachers. The impact of the new perception will therefore be necessarily varied, but probably beneficial in most cases, since even its rejection will have involved a re-examination – hence a heightened awareness – of an existing one. Also, the impact in all cases is likely to be a modification (rather than a replacement) of existing perceptions, even when the modification leads to a close approximation to the new perception.

To the extent that there is an activation or a modification of a teacher's pedagogic perception, there is likely to be a corresponding change in the balance of forces which constitutes his or her 'mental mix', the new balance generally representing a larger role for the pedagogic perception in relation to the other forces. As a result, there is a greater probability of satisfaction or dissatisfaction deriving from teaching routines and a greater chance of their being gradually modified in the direction of the pattern of classroom activity suggested by the innovation. Again, the changes in teaching routines will necessarily be varied in nature, extent, and speed. The modified routines will, however, not be mere routines (since the modifications were prompted by changing pedagogic perceptions) and both perceptions and routines are now likely to be more open to further change than they were earlier.

Statutory implementation of an innovation, by contrast, is likely to distort all these processes and aggravate the tensions in teachers' mental frames. The threat to existing routines can make many teachers reject the innovation out of hand, as an act of self-protection. Alternatively, a strong sense of plausibility about some existing perception may make some teachers see the innovation as counter-intuitive and look on its implementation as pedagogically harmful. If rejection itself appears to be too great a risk (in view of acceptance by colleagues or official sponsorship) teachers may take on the new routines while rejecting the perception behind them, thus making them mere routines from the beginning. Or they may dissociate perception from practice, operating with the perception in contexts in which perceptions are seen to be relevant, such as professional discussion, but operating without it in the classroom. Some teachers may accept the innovation on trust, others in the expectation of some reward, yet others as an escape from existing problems of security or routinization, yet others for reasons of self-image or personal ideology. While statutory implementation is likely, when successful, to achieve a large measure of conformity to new teaching routines, it is also likely to reduce the possible impact of the new perception and its potential for stimulating teacher development.[1]

The underlying assumption of statutory implementation is that the value of an innovation lies in the pattern of teaching activity it leads to, independently of the perception which informed that innovation, and that the value can be realized even when the pattern of activity is carried out without any engagement of the teacher's sense of plausibility. A new method is thus seen as a set of classroom procedures which carry a 'guarantee' of learning outcomes when carried out as specified. In arguing against statutory implementation, it is being suggested here that teaching procedures are of value in the classroom only to the extent they are informed by relevant perceptions, and that teaching is too complex an activity for there to be any objective procedures with guaranteed outcomes. A good system of education, from this point of view, is not one in which all or most teachers carry out the same recommended classroom procedures but rather a system in which (1) all, or most, teachers operate with a sense of plausibility about whatever procedures they choose to adopt, and (2) each teacher's sense of plausibility is as 'alive' or active, and hence as open to further development or change as it can be.[2]

When the teacher's sense of plausibility is engaged in classroom activity and the activity has, at the same time, the support of a stable routine, there is both a sense of security provided by the routine and also a feeling of there being something at stake: each lesson is a new event, unpredictably satisfying or disappointing, despite its being largely a matter of routine. This can lead to a form of rapport between the teacher and learners, enabling each to interpret the intentions of the other and to respond in the knowledge that the response has a role in shaping the activity in progress. This rapport represents a form of empathetic understanding of each other's behaviour and is probably more productive of learning than any teaching procedure by itself can be.[3]

Language teaching specialism

From this point of view, language teaching specialism ('applied linguistics' in one sense of the term) is a matter of identifying, developing, and articulating particular perceptions of teaching and learning on the one hand, and seeking ways in which perceptions can be shared and sharpened through professional debate in the teaching community on the other.[4] Without this professional debate, a teacher has only classroom experience to draw on – and the pressures towards routinization in teaching are such that the classroom can easily cease to be a source of interpretable experience. Participation in debate can activate intuitions, bring about interaction with different perceptions, and help to develop a sense of plausibility capable of guiding as well as drawing on classroom experience. Particular perceptions represent interpretations of experience; and they are defined and articulated by drawing on one or more related disciplines as sources of illuminative constructs, by relating them to other perceptions developed elsewhere or at other times, and perhaps by deliberately seeking corroboration and clarification in the classroom or in focused debate. The teaching procedures suggested by a perception help to make it accessible and available for further corroboration, development, or change through further classroom experience. What procedures a teacher follows in the classroom depends on what perception he or she sees most plausibility in, and the impact of any perception on classrooms depends on its ability to invoke corroborative intuitions in the teaching community.[5]

Eclecticism

The fact that pedagogic perceptions vary both among specialists and among teachers is sometimes taken to be an argument for some form of eclecticism in language teaching. It is, however, not clear what eclecticism consists of and how it operates. There seem to be at least four distinguishable concepts involved:

1 Eclecticism is a matter of operating with a combination of perceptions or procedures which, though all different and some perhaps arguably inconsistent with others, have nevertheless found a satisfying balance in the mind of an individual. In this sense, what was referred to above as the teacher's 'mental mix' is eclectic, as is to some extent the conceptual framework of every proposal in pedagogy (and indeed every individual's view of the world).

2 Eclecticism is an exercise of worldly wisdom – a search for the safest course in the midst of many risks. An adviser who has responsibility for making recommendations for large-scale change in pedagogy adopts strategies such as identifying the common ground in the specialist field, distributing risks, and making concessions to practical or sentimental needs. He or she sees this role as one of mediating between the specialism and the teaching community, and regards the work as being eclectic.

3 Eclecticism is a desirable principle of life. It is a refusal to see things in terms of irreconcilable alternatives and a belief that, where there are alternative courses of action available, the 'right' course must be somewhere between the two.

4 Eclecticism is the development of a new perception which enables one to see earlier perceptions in a new light or a new relationship, thus resolving what was earlier seen as a conflict. This is what often happens when there is a shift in focus which renders earlier dichotomies irrelevant or reveals earlier interpretations as having been inadequate.

The second of these concepts relates to the context of statutory implementation, which has been argued against in this chapter. The third is not specifically related to pedagogy and not open to examination at the level of this discussion. Only the first and the last are relevant, but the difference between the two can be regarded as being only a matter of explicitness: if different perceptions have found a satisfying balance in a teacher's mind, that balance constitutes his or her dormant pedagogic intuition which is available for articulation and which, when articulated, can represent a new relationship between the earlier perceptions. The process of articulating such dormant intuitions deserves a central role in pedagogic innovation and in the maintenance of what may be called teachers' 'professional activism'.

There appears to occur from time to time, and in different places and contexts, a convergence of similar pedagogic perceptions, or a convergence of corroborative responses to the same perception. Such convergence leads to a stable 'paradigm' of perception and practice over a period of time and may be regarded as evidence of a perception's validity, i.e. its power to invoke wide corroboration. However, this stability can promote an over-routinization of classroom practice, causing a gradual weakening or loss of the sense of plausibility about the original perception. Pedagogic innovation in such a situation may be viewed as an act of renewing contact with intuition and re-interpreting experience through a fresh perception.

The project in India was essentially an attempt to develop a fresh perception of second language teaching and learning. It drew on a pedagogic intuition arising from earlier experience, and deliberately sought further sustained experience, both to test the strength of the intuition and to be able to articulate it in the form of principles and procedures. As described in Chapter 2, the project arose in the context of a loss of plausibility to the perception behind the prevailing S-O-S pedagogy, and drew on the stimulus provided, at the time, by some of the proposals for communicative language teaching.[5] How the project's initial intuition came to be articulated in the form of teaching procedures, teaching principles, and hypothesized learning processes was described in Chapters 3, 4, and 5. As the perspective on pedagogic change outlined in this final chapter will have indicated, my intention in presenting this description is to make the perception developed on the project available for corroboration, criticism, and interaction with other perceptions in the profession, perhaps resulting in the development of further perceptions.

Notes

1 It is common to interpret this phenomenon as a failure on the part of teachers to understand the theory behind the new method – and to seek ways of making the method 'easy to follow', i.e. a matter of well-defined routine, which is easy to carry out as mere routine.

2 See Fenstermacher (1982) for a similar view of the relationship between educational research and teacher effectiveness. Fenstermacher argues that research is best passed on to teachers in the form of schemata – 'a way to see a phenomenon and a way to think about it' – thus providing teachers with 'the means to structure their experience with the classroom'.

3 It is this empathetic understanding which seems to me to represent what is referred to as 'knowing teaching from the inside'. See, for instance, the discussion in Brumfit (1984a:5–7).

4 See Widdowson (1980). For Widdowson, however, even the pedagogically relevant sense of 'applied linguistics' has to do with developing models of *language description* relevant to pedagogy.

5 As mentioned in Chapter 1, note 5, at the time it was set up the project did not have access to other proposals relevant to its thinking, such as those of promoting acquisition through comprehensible input (Krashen 1981), delaying production in the early stages of instruction (Winitz 1981), and, most significantly, viewing language development as a sequence of transitional competences (Corder 1981). However, these proposals did have an influence on the articulation of the project's perceptions at later stages and I think they indicate a measure of convergence of perceptions at the present time.

Bibliography

Allen, J. P. B. and H. G. Widdowson. 1974. *English in Focus: English in Physical Science*. Oxford: Oxford University Press.

Allwright, R. L. 1976. 'Syllabus design and evaluation' in *UCLA Workbook on TESL Methodology*. Los Angeles, CA: University of California at Los Angeles.

Allwright, R. L. 1981. 'What do we want teaching materials for?' *ELT Journal* 36/1:5–18.

Beretta, A. and A. Davies. 1985. 'Evaluation of the Bangalore Project.' *ELT Journal* 29/2:121–7. (Reproduced as Appendix VI in this book.)

Bialystok, E. 1978. 'A theoretical model of second language learning.' *Language Learning* 28/1:69–83.

Bialystok, E. 1983. 'Inferencing: testing the "hypothesis-testing" hypothesis' in H. Seliger and M. H. Long (eds.). *Classroom-Oriented Research*, Rowley, Mass.: Newbury House.

Bloomfield, L. 1914. *An Introduction to the Study of Language*. London: G. Bell and Sons.

Brown, R. 1973. *A First Language: The Early Stages*. London: George Allen and Unwin.

Brumfit, C. J. 1984a. *Communicative Methodology in Language Teaching*. Cambridge: Cambridge University Press.

Brumfit, C. J. 1984b. 'The Bangalore Procedural Syllabus.' *ELT Journal* 38/4:233–41.

Brumfit, C. J. (ed.) 1984c. *General English Syllabus Design* (ELT Documents 118). Oxford: Pergamon Press for the British Council.

Chomsky, N. 1976. *Reflections on Language*. London: Temple Smith.

Chomsky, N. 1979. *Language and Responsibility*. Brighton: Harvester.

Chomsky, N. 1980. *Rules and Representations*. Oxford: Basil Blackwell.

Collingham, M. 1981. 'Teaching techniques in task-based learning.' MA dissertation, University of Lancaster.

Corder, S. P. 1981. *Error Analysis and Interlanguage*. Oxford: Oxford University Press.

Davies, A., C. Criper, and A. P. R. Howatt (eds.). 1984. *Interlanguage*. Edinburgh: Edinburgh University Press.

Donaldson, M. 1978. *Children's Minds*. London: Collins/Fontana.

van Ek, J. A. 1975. *The Threshold Level*. Strasbourg: Council of Europe.

Ericson, D. P. and F. S. Ellett. 1982. 'Interpretation, understanding and evaluational research.' *Teachers' College Record* 83/4: 497–513.

Fenstermacher, G. D. 1982. 'On learning to teach effectively from research on teacher effectiveness.' *Evaluational Researcher* 17/2.

Frawley, W. and **J. Lantolf.** 1985. 'Second language discourse: A Vigotskyan perspective.' *Applied Linguistics* 6/1:19–44.

Gilpin, A. 1981. 'The influence of the teacher's method on the pre-task phase of problem-solving tasks.' MA dissertation, University of Lancaster.

Greenwood, J. 1985. 'Bangalore revisited: a reluctant complaint.' *ELT Journal* 39/4: 268–73.

Howatt, A. P. R. 1984. *A History of English Language Teaching.* Oxford: Oxford University Press.

Johnson, K. and **K. Morrow.** 1979. *Approaches.* Cambridge: Cambridge University Press.

Johnson, K. 1982. *Communicative Syllabus Design and Methodology.* Oxford: Pergamon Press.

Krashen, S. 1981. *Second Language Acquisition and Second Language Learning.* Oxford: Pergamon Press.

Krashen, S. 1982. *Principles and Practice in Second Language Acquisition.* Oxford: Pergamon Press.

Krashen, S. and **T. Terrell.** 1983. *The Natural Approach.* Hayward, California: Alemany Press.

Kumaravadivelu, B. 1981. 'Turn organisation in L1 and L2 classroom discourse.' MA dissertation, University of Lancaster.

Mizon, S. 1981. 'Teacher talk.' MA dissertation, University of Lancaster.

Morrow, K. and **K. Johnson.** 1979. *Communicate.* Cambridge: Cambridge University Press.

Nagpur Report. 1958. *The Teaching of English in Secondary Schools: Report of the All India Seminar of Lecturers of Secondary Training Colleges, Nagpur, from December 5 to December 20, 1957.* New Delhi: All India Council for Secondary Education.

Naiman, N., M. Frolich, H. Stern, and **A. Todesco.** 1978. *The Good Language Learner. Research in Education Series No. 7.* Toronto: Ontario Institute for Studies in Education.

Palmer, H. E. 1917. *The Scientific Study and Teaching of Languages.* London: Harrap. (Republished by Oxford University Press, 1968, edited by D. Harper.)

Palmer, H. E. 1921. *The Oral Method of Teaching Languages.* Cambridge: Heffer.

Pickett, G. D. 1978. *The Foreign Language Learning Process.* (ETIC Occasional Papers) London: The British Council.

Prabhu, N. S. 1979. 'The teaching of English and notions about communication' in Jack C. Richards (ed.), *Application of Linguistics to Language Teaching* (RELC Anthology Series 6). Singapore: Singapore

University Press.

Rajan, S. 1983. 'A critique of the Communicational Teaching Project.' MA dissertation, University of London Institute of Education.

Richards, J. C. 1984. 'The secret life of methods.' *TESOL Quarterly* 18/1: 7–23.

RIE Bulletin, Special Series No. 2. 1978. Bangalore: Regional Institute of English.

RIE Bulletin No. 3. 1979. Bangalore: Regional Institute of English.

RIE Bulletin No. 4(i). 1980a. Bangalore: Regional Institute of English.

RIE Bulletin No. 4(ii). 1980b. Bangalore: Regional Institute of English.

RIE Bulletin No. 5(i). 1981. Bangalore: Regional Institute of English.

Rubin, J. 1975. 'What the "good language learner" can teach us.' *TESOL Quarterly* 9/1:41–51.

Saraswathi, V. 1984. 'The Communicational Teaching Project: an evaluation' MSc dissertation, University of Edinburgh.

Smith, D. A. 1962. 'The Madras Snowball: an attempt to retrain 27,000 teachers of English to beginners.' *ELT Journal* 17/1: 3–9.

Smith, D. A. 1968. 'In-service training for teachers of English in developing countries' in Perren G. E. (ed.) *Teachers of English as a Second Language.* Cambridge: Cambridge University Press.

Study Group Report. 1967. *The Study of English in India.* New Delhi: Government of India Ministry of Education.

Study Group Report. 1971. *The Teaching of English.* New Delhi: Government of India Ministry of Education and Youth Services.

Swain, M. and S. Lapkin. 1982. *Evaluating Bilingual Education: A Canadian Case Study.* Clevedon: Multilingual Matters Ltd.

Vigotsky, L. S. 1978. *Mind in Society: The Development of Higher Psychological Processes.* Cambridge, Mass.: Harvard University Press.

Widdowson, H. G. 1968. 'The Teaching of English Through Science' in J. Dakin, B. Tiffen, and H. G. Widdowson (eds.) *Language in Education.* Oxford: Oxford University Press.

Widdowson, H. G. 1978. *Teaching Language as Communication.* Oxford: Oxford University Press.

Widdowson, H. G. 1980. 'Models and fictions.' *Applied Linguistics* 1/2:165–9.

Widdowson, H. G. 1983. *Learning Purpose and Language Use.* Oxford: Oxford University Press.

Wilkins, D. A. 1976. *Notional Syllabuses.* Oxford: Oxford University Press.

Wilkins, D. A. 1981. 'Notional Syllabuses revisited: a further reply.' *Applied Linguistics* 2/1:96–100.

Winitz, H. (ed.) 1981. *The Comprehension Approach to Foreign Language Instruction.* Rowley, Mass.: Newbury House.

Descriptions of S-O-S pedagogy
Appendix Ia

A report in *The Indian Express* of 13 April 1960: 'Learning English Without Tears' by our Staff Reporter, New Delhi

'This is a pencil. . . . This is a book. . . . This is a flower. This is a red pencil. . . . This is a red book. . . . This is a red flower. The pencil is on the book. The red pencil is on the book.'

The teacher, holding aloft one by one pencils, books and flowers of various colours, went on repeating each sentence and the little girls in the class spoke after him. Within a few minutes, some of them were even able to repeat the sentences, without the help of the teacher.

The wonder about it was that only a few minutes earlier none of the girls knew even a word of English. They were now able to speak a few sentences and knew what they conveyed.

Still more surprising, this was achieved without the teacher having to use a single Hindi word to make himself understood.

New system

The teacher was Mr U. who was giving at the M.C. Higher Secondary School, Rouse Avenue, a demonstration of how to teach English according to a new system, the structural-situational method, which is the other name for learning English without tears.

Revolutionary in its approach, the new system straightaway starts teaching the child the complete sentence. The alphabet comes much later.

The system is designed to teach English to children in the same way they learn their mother tongue.

This new system has already found much support. It has been recommended by the UNESCO for use in teaching foreign languages. It is at present being taught in schools in Indonesia, Burma and East Pakistan.

The schools of the Delhi Corporation will switch over to this system from the next term, beginning on July 15, in the sixth class.

Avoiding confusion

The new system deserves wide publicity for if parents and private tutors continue to teach students at home according to the old system and the Delhi schools switch over to the new system, the children will be subjected to much confusion. A guide book has been prepared for teachers and another for students. The Corporation teachers are being trained at present under the auspices of the Study Circle of English Teachers of the Corporation, with the assistance of the British Council.

The old system of beginning with the alphabet has been criticised as an 'approach completely divorced from life's situations'. People who follow this method may become masters of the theory of language but they cannot use it as a vehicle of communication for satisfying their everyday needs, it is said.

It has been proved by language experts that learning of individual words is not of much importance in the learning of English as a foreign language. In the new system, the sentence, and not the word or the letter, is treated as a unit.

Vocabulary

People who follow the new system say if the vocabulary is taught through graded sentence structures used in actual situations, the learning of the language becomes easier. It is a waste of time, they say, to teach the alphabet to beginners. The learning of a word is as difficult or as easy for young minds as the learning of a letter. Since English is not a phonetic language, the new system also eliminates pronunciation difficulties.

The system rests on one main assumption, that the sentence is the unit of the language. If the sentence is taught straightaway, there is no need to teach the grammatical terminology in the beginning.

Although the alphabet is not taught in the beginning in the new system, the students learn to get acquainted with the written word. This was also demonstrated by Mr U. He sketched a pencil, a book and a flower on the blackboard and, as earlier, made the students repeat after him 'this is a pencil' and so on. Next, under each figure he wrote out the respective word for it. After the students had considerable practice and could associate the respective figures and words written beneath them, he rubbed off the figures. The students could read the words without any difficulty, although they did not know a single letter. The new system seeks to acquaint the student with the word as a 'complete block by itself'.

A barrier

Mr U. emphasized that it was not necessary to teach English with the aid of the mother-tongue. In fact, he positively discouraged the practice. The teacher, he said, should always speak in the language he was trying to teach. In the English class the teacher should always speak in English, without having to resort to mental translation, which was a barrier to fluency. 'Teaching with the help of translation is a pointless waste of time', he said.

According to Mr U., a beginner can learn 600 words in one year by following the new system. The syllabus, however, provides for only 240 words to be learnt. A great advantage in this system is that the students can start learning the use of the preposition and the article from the very beginning.

In order to enable the child to enjoy the sensation of beginning to be able to express ideas and to avoid boredom, the lessons should be short, preferably not of more than half an hour's duration.

There is little doubt that the new method can succeed only if the teachers approach the students 'gently and patiently' – as was brilliantly displayed by Mr U. himself in his lecture-demonstration. His approach all along was to help the child to speak up and not to be constantly putting his understanding to test.

Appendix Ib

A report, made by S. Durairaj in March 1965, on observable classroom effects of in-service teacher training in S-O-S pedagogy: 'Procedures in teaching the structures "the green line is very long, the white one is very short"'.

Teacher A

Draws first a horizontal green line on the blackboard as long as possible and then another white line about six inches long. Says 'The green line is very long, the white one is very short'. Rubs the line out and, giving a piece of green chalk to a pupil, commands 'Draw a very long line on the blackboard'. Rubs it out and gives the same command to one or more pupils. Then, rubbing the line out each time and giving a piece of white chalk to a pupil, commands him to draw a very short line. This action is repeated in the case of several boys.

Teacher then draws a very long green line and a very short white line, and asks:

Teacher Is the green line very long?
Pupils Yes, it is.
Teacher Is the green line very short?
Pupils No, it isn't.
Teacher Is the white line very long?
Pupils No, it isn't.
Teacher Which line is very long? – The green one is.

Teacher repeats the question and answer several times and then asks the pupils:

Teacher Which line is very long?
Pupils The green one is.
Teacher Which one is very short?
Pupils The white one is.

Then teacher uses the same procedures again but uses, instead, coloured pieces of string and ribbon, and sticks, some of them very long, and some very short. As pupils give the answers, the teacher works out the following substitution table on the blackboard and uses it for practice in reading and writing:

The	blue yellow red green white	line stick piece of	 ribbon string cloth	is	very long very short

Teacher B

Teacher B uses the same aids as those used by teacher A (i.e. coloured lines, sticks, and pieces of ribbon) but asks the specific question as soon as she makes the statements:

Teacher The red line/stick is very long. Which line/stick is very long?

Teacher gives the answer and pupils repeat it.

Teacher The white line/stick is very short. Which line/stick is very short?

Teacher then puts these sentences on the blackboard and gets pupils to read them first and then copy them into their exercise books.

Teacher C

Gets pupils to open their texts. Reads out the following sentences: 'The green line is very long, the white one is very short.' Then he draws a very long green line and a very short white line, moves his finger along each line as he says: 'The green line is very long, the white one is very short'. Then he gets all children to repeat after him the two sentences as he runs his stick or finger along the two lines. Then he gets each pupil to go to the blackboard, run his finger along the lines and repeat the sentences. Then teacher reads the two sentences from the text and passes on to teach the next sentence in the text.

Comments on the procedures adopted

These three procedures represent a fair cross section of Campaign teaching potential, with teacher A reflecting the best, and teacher C just the minimum.

All three of them conform to the spirit of the Campaign in the sense that they:
- use situations to introduce new language
- provide for speech, reading, and writing while teaching a new structure
- teach reading a sentence after pupils have learnt to say it
- avoid the use of the mother tongue.

Teacher C depends solely on the sentences given in the course book, monotonous repetitive drill of a single sentence, and statements (note that he asks no questions).

Teacher B is less rigid and contrives more than one situation to introduce the new language. She and her children open the coursebook only after pupils are familiar with the new pattern. Though she uses questions to a certain extent, she does not lead pupils up to answer the specific questions.

Teacher A is very resourceful and imaginative; uses a variety of situations; makes use of commands and recognition questions to facilitate comprehension; leads up naturally to the specific question; makes drills more interesting by concentrating on the pattern rather than on a single sentence; uses the substitution table for two purposes; provides for revision of vocabulary learnt earlier (e.g. names of colours and objects).

Conclusions

It is evident that:
- all Campaign-trained teachers are aware of the importance of speech before reading and writing
- the effectiveness of a teacher in the classroom depends as much on the resourcefulness and personality of the teacher as on Campaign methodology.

Appendix II
Initial perceptions of the project

January 1978

Broadly, semantic syllabuses promise two things: (1) an extension of the area of competence that is imparted to learners – i.e. an extension beyond grammatical competence, to include (at least some aspects of) what has been called 'communicative competence'; and (2) a reorientation of methodology, with the aim of keeping the learner preoccupied with (some form of) meaning while he learns – much less consciously than he does under present procedures – the forms of language and their abstract relationships. . . . However, [a semantic syllabus] inevitably destroys the systematicity of structural progression on a course. One hopes that the methodology that goes with a semantic syllabus (namely, learners' preoccupation with meaning) will make up for such a loss of structural systematicity, but it might be advisable to satisfy oneself that it does, before launching a new syllabus. (*RIE Bulletin, Special Series No. 2, 1978: 33, 35*)

April 1978

We thus have something of a paradoxical situation, as follows: (1) courses based on grammatical structure often fail to achieve their aim of imparting grammatical competence; (2) it is now realised that learners need to go beyond grammatical competence to acquire communicative competence; and (3) teaching for communicative competence necessarily involves less systematic teaching of grammatical structure (and therefore appears less likely to succeed in imparting grammatical competence).

Some suggestions have appeared in the literature on possible ways of reconciling grammatical and semantic organisations . . . [but] I think there is a basic claim, made hesitantly, in such proposals, namely, that the linguistic code is learnt better if, in the process of learning it, learners' attention is not on the code itself but on some problem of meaning or message involving the use of the code. There is a parallel here to the essential claim that was involved in the earlier transition from language teaching through rules of grammar to merely the presentation and practice of (sets of) similar sentences: the claim was that the rules of grammar are learnt ('internalised') better if, in the process of learning them, attention is not on the rules but on the actual forms which exemplify them. . . . There is thus, from this point of view, a progression from explicit grammar (in the classroom) to exemplificatory forms alone to meaning and use – from a direct learning of the theory (i.e. grammar) to its indirect aquisition through evidence to an indirect perception of the evidence itself. (*Prabhu 1979: 78–9*)

July 1979

A language teaching approach is concerned primarily with (1) a view of what is being taught and (2) a consensus on how it is best taught. . . . In the Communicational Approach here being investigated, what is taught is seen in terms of both language structure (i.e. the rules of 'usage') and language use (i.e. the employment in successful communication of the rules learnt). We believe this to be best taught by bringing about in the learner a preoccupation with meaning or with a task to be performed, resulting in a desire on his part to communicate. . . . The Working Group feels that this perception of how language is best taught is the most distinctive characteristic of this approach, the addition of 'use' under 'what' being almost a consequence of this methodological principle. . . . The new methodological principle should stand or fall by its success in achieving an internalization of structure. (*RIE Newsletter 1/1, 1979: 1–2*)

September 1979

We adopt of necessity what may be called an 'eclipsing view': the view that what we are hypothesising is the 'whole truth' – that communicational activity, which we are trying to define, evolve and test the result of, is *all* that is needed in language teaching. It is only by taking such a stance (and acting accordingly) that we can find out *how much* such activity can achieve. (*RIE Newsletter 1/2, 1979: 21–2*)

Appendix III
Schools involved in the project

Government Girls' High School, Malleswaram, Bangalore 560 012

Corporation Girls' High School, Nungambakkam, Madras 600 034

Sri R.K.M. Sarada Vidyalaya Middle School, T. Nagar, Madras 600 017

Corporation Boys' High School, Tasker Town, Bangalore 560 052

Sacred Heart's School, Cuddalore, South Arcot District, Tamil Nadu

St Anthony's Kannada Upgraded Primary School, Jayanagar T-Block, Bangalore 560 041

Vellayan Chettiar Higher Secondary School, Tiruvottiyur, Madras 600 019

Transcripts of project lessons
Appendix IVa

Transcript of the pre-task stages of a lesson taught on 2 March 1981 to a class of forty eleven-year-olds who were in their fourth year of English but in the first year of project teaching. See Chapter 2, pages 31–3 for a general description of this lesson. This transcript was made by A. Gilpin and B. Kumaravadivelu.

Teacher   Good morning, children.
Students   Good morning, sir.

(Preliminary pre-task)

Teacher   Sit down. Look at that. (*The teacher writes '0600 hours = 6 a.m.' on the blackboard.*) Zero six zero zero hours. That means . . .
Students   Six a.m.
Teacher   Now, what does this mean? Zero six three zero hours. (*The teacher writes '0630'.*)
Students   Six thirty p.m.
Teacher   Six thirty . . .? (*pause*)
Students   p.m.
Teacher   Six thirty . . .? (*pause*)
Students   a.m.
Teacher   a.m. . . . . yes. (*pause*) Zero eight zero zero hours. (*The teacher writes '0800'.*)
Students   Eight a.m.
Teacher   Eight a.m. (*pause*) Now, next question. Don't give the answer. Just put up your hands. Zero nine one five . . . (*The teacher writes '0915'.*) Whom shall we ask? Uh . . . (*indicates student 1*)
Student 1   Nine – nine – nine fifteen a.m.
Teacher   Nine fifteen a.m. Yes, good . . . One one four five. (*The teacher writes '1145'.*) Eleven four five hours.
Students   (*indistinct*)
Teacher   Say it again.
Student   Eleven forty-five.

Teacher	Eleven forty-five . . . ?
Student	Umm . . . a.m.
Students	p.m. . . . a.m.
Teacher	a.m. yes, good. (*pause*) One two zero zero . . . (*The teacher writes '1200'.*)
Student	Twelve.
Teacher	Twelve, do we say a.m.?
Students	p.m. . . . noon.
Student	Afternoon.
Teacher	Twelve noon, yes. Now, one three zero zero hours. (*The teacher writes '1300'.*)
Student	One thirty a.m. . . .
Students	p.m.
Teacher	One . . . thirty . . .
Student	p.m.
Teacher	p.m. (*indicates student 2*)
Student 2	One thirty
Teacher	One thirty . . .
Student 2	p.m.
Teacher	p.m. . . . (*indicates student 3*)
Student 3	One p.m.
Teacher	One p.m.
Student 4	One p.m.
Teacher	One p.m.
Students	One thirty p.m.
Teacher	One thirty p.m.?
Students	One p.m.
Teacher	One p.m. is correct. (*The teacher writes '12 noon' and '1 p.m.'*) Twelve noon, thirteen. One hour more. Zero zero . . . how many? Right. One p.m. Now, one five zero zero hours. (*The teacher writes '1500'. After a pause, he indicates student 5.*)
Student 5	Three p.m.
Teacher	Three p.m.
Students	One forty-five p.m.
Teacher	One forty-five . . .
Students	One forty-five . . .
Students	One forty p.m.
Teacher	One forty p.m. Yes?
Students	Three p.m.
Teacher	Three p.m. (*indicates student 1*)
Student 1	Three p.m.

Teacher	Three p.m. (*After a pause, the teacher indicates student 2.*)
Student 2	Three p.m.
Teacher	Yes, three p.m. Correct. (*The teacher writes '3 p.m.'*) Three p.m. Twelve . . . fifteen . . . three . . . uh . . . one eight zero zero (*The teacher writes '1800'.*) One, two, three, four, five, six, seven, eight . . . (*The teacher counts the number of students who put up their hands and then indicates student 6.*)
Student 6	Three p.m.
Teacher	Eighteen . . . uh . . . three p.m. (*After a pause, the teacher indicates student 7.*)
Student 7	Six p.m.
Teacher	(*indicates student 5*)
Student 5	Six p.m.
Teacher	(*indicates student 8*)
Student 8	Six p.m.
Teacher	p.m. (*indicates student 4*)
Student 4	Six p.m.
Teacher	Six p.m. . . . . Yes, how do you know?
Student 4	Eighteen minus twelve.
Teacher	Eighteen minus twelve . . . after twelve . . . six more . . . six p.m. Good. Now, it's going to be a little difficult . . . twenty one five hours. (*The teacher writes '2015'.*) Who can give the answer? One, two, three, four, five, six, seven . . . (*indicates student 9*)
Student 9	Eight fifteen a.m.
Teacher	Eight fifteen, a.m. Eight fifteen, a.m. . . . ? (*indicates student 3*)
Student 3	Eight fifteen, p.m. . . .
Teacher	(*indicates student 9*)
Student 9	Eight fifteen p.m.
Teacher	Eight fifteen, p.m. is correct. (*The teacher writes '8.15 p.m.'*) Now, it's going to be *very* difficult. Zero zero zero zero hours. (*The teacher writes '0000'.*) Who can give me the answer? Selvi . . . Alamelu . . . uh . . . yes?
Alamelu	Zero p.m.
Students	(*laugh*)
Teacher	Zero p.m. . . . . (*indicates student 4*)
Student 4	No hours.
Teacher	No hours . . . (*indicates student 5*)
Student 5	No hours.

Teacher	No hours . . . *(indicates student 2)*
Student 2	No hours.
Teacher	No hours . . . Well, actually it means twenty-four.
Student	Twenty-four?
Teacher	Twenty four. What does twenty-four mean?
Student	Twelve p.m. One day.
Teacher	Twelve.
Student	p.m.
Teacher	Twelve p.m.
Student	Twelve night . . . noon?
Teacher	Midnight. Yes, twelve midnight, yes twelve midnight here . . . the day . . . twelve noon . . . there midnight. Now, zero one four five hours. What does that mean? *(The teacher writes '0145'.)* One, two, three, four . . . yes?
Student	One forty-five p.m.
Student	One forty-five . . . one forty-five . . .
Student	p.m.
Teacher	Not p.m.
Students	a.m.
Teacher	a.m. . . . yes a.m. This is the last. Zero four one five hours. *(The teacher writes '0415'. After a pause, he indicates student 10.)*
Student 10	Four . . .
Teacher	Four . . .
Student 10	. . . fifteen a.m.
Teacher	Four fifteen a.m. Four fifteen a.m. yes, good.

(Pre-task – preliminary 'task' omitted)

	(The teacher writes the timetable for the Brindavan Express on the board.) That is Brindavan Express which goes from Madras to Bangalore. Where does it stop on the way?
Students	Katpadi.
Teacher	Katpadi and . . .
Students	Jolarpet.
Teacher	Jolarpet, yes. What time does it leave Madras?
Students	Seven twenty-five a.m.
Teacher	Seven twenty-five . . .
Students	. . . a.m.
Teacher	Yes, seven twenty-five a.m. What time does it arrive in Bangalore?

Students	Nine. . . . One
Teacher	What time does it arrive . . .
Students	(*severally*) One p.m. . . . One thirty p.m. . . . One p.m.
Teacher	Who says one p.m.? . . . Who says one thirty p.m.? (*pause*) Not one thirty p.m. One p.m. is correct. One p.m. When does it arrive in Katpadi?
Students	Nine fifteen a.m. . . . Nine fifteen a.m.
Teacher	. . . arrive . . . arrive in Katpadi.
Students	Nine fifteen a.m.
Teacher	Nine fifteen a.m. Correct. . . . When does it leave Jolarpet? Don't give the answer, put up your hands. When does it leave Jolarpet? When does it leave Jolarpet? When does it leave Jolarpet? . . . When does it leave Jolarpet? (*pause*) Any more . . .? (*indicates student 11*)
Student 11	Ten thirty p.m.
Teacher	Leaves Jolarpet at ten thirty . . .
Student 11	a.m.
Teacher	a.m. Yes. Ten thirty a.m. correct. . . . Now, you have to listen carefully. For how long . . . for how long does it *stop* at Katpadi? How long is the *stop* in Katpadi? . . . (*indicates student 4*)
Student 4	Five minutes.
Teacher	Five minutes, yes. How do you know?
Student	Twenty . . .
Student 4	Twenty minus fifteen.
Teacher	Fifteen . . . nine fifteen arrival, nine twenty departure . . . twenty minus fifteen, five, yes. . . . How long is the stop at Jolarpet? How long is the stop at Jolarpet? (*After a pause, the teacher indicates student 12.*)
Student 12	Two minutes.
Teacher	Two minutes, yes. Thirty minus twenty-eight, two minutes, yes correct. Now we shall listen again carefully. How long does it take . . . how long does the train take to go from Madras to Katpadi? How long does it take to go from Madras to Katpadi? . . . to go from Madras to Katpadi? (*pause*) It's difficult. You have to calculate. (*After another pause, the teacher indicates student 2.*)
Student 2	Two hours.
Teacher	Two hours. Any other answer? (*indicates student 4*)
Student 4	Two ten.

Teacher	Two ten. (*indicates student 12*)
Student 12	Two hours ten minutes.
Teacher	Two hours ten minutes. Any other answers? (*pause*) Yes? (*indicates student 13*)
Student 13	Two hours, uh . . . five . . . five . . . five minutes.
Teacher	Two hours five minutes . . . uh . . . no, that's not the answer. No. Any other answer? (*pause*) If it is two hours, if it is two hours, what time should it arrive in Katpadi?
Students	Nine fifteen.
Teacher	Nine . . .
Students	Fifteen.
Teacher	If it is two hours? It leaves at nine twenty-five . . . seven twenty-five, sorry. It leaves at seven twenty-five. If it is two hours when should it arrive here?
Students	Nine fifteen.
Teacher	Nine . . .
Students	. . . fifteen.
Teacher	Add two hours to seven twenty-five . . . (*pause*) seven twenty-five . . .
Students	Four hours.
Teacher	No, add two hours to seven twenty-five . . . (*pause*) seven twenty-five and then two hours.
Student	Eight . . .
Teacher	Eight twenty-five?
Students	Nine twenty-five.
Teacher	Nine twenty-five it should arrive at Katpadi. When does it arrive in Katpadi?
Students	Nine fifteen.
Teacher	Nine fifteen, *before* that. So, is it less than two hours or more?
Student	Less.
Teacher	Less, less than two hours, yes. Now . . . (*indicates student 3*)
Student 3	Two fifteen, two fifteen.
Teacher	Two hours fifteen minutes, no. It's less than two hours. One hour and some minutes. How many minutes?
Students	Fifteen. . . . One fifty.
Teacher	One hour and yes . . .
Student	One fifty.
Teacher	One hour and fifty minutes. Yes, correct. One hour and fifty minutes. One hour and fifty minutes. (*The teacher*

writes '1 hour and 50 minutes'.) If it is two hours, it will be nine twenty-five. Nine fifteen. Ten minutes less. One hour and fifty, ten minutes less than one hour . . . . All right. The next question. How long does it take to go from Madras to Jolarpet? Madras to Jolarpet. How long does the train take to go from Madras to Jolarpet . . . (*After a pause, the teacher indicates student 2.*)

Student 2	Ten hours three minutes, ten hours three minutes.
Teacher	Ten hours and three minutes. Ten hours?
Student 2	Three.
Teacher	Three hours and yes – yes . . .
Students	. . . three minutes.
Teacher	Three hours and three minutes. That's correct. Three hours and three minutes. If it is three hours, seven twenty-five, eight twenty-five, nine twenty-five, ten twenty-five. Ten twenty-eight. Three more minutes. Three hours and three minutes. Right. . . . (*pause*) How many stations . . . how many stations does the train stop at, on the way? On the way from Madras to Bangalore, how many stations does it stop at? How many?
Student	Four stations.
Teacher	Four stations.
Student	Two stations.
Teacher	Two stations. (*indicates student 3*)
Student 3	Two stations.
Teacher	Two stations. (*indicates student 4*)
Student 4	Two stations.
Teacher	Two stations. (*indicates student 2*)
Student 2	Two stations.
Teacher	(*indicates student 7*)
Student 7	Two stations.
Teacher	Two stations, yes. Which stations does it stop at, on the way?
Students	Katpadi, Jolarpet.
Teacher	Katpadi and Jolarpet. Madras is the starting station, Bangalore is the station it arrives at in the end. On the way it stops at two stations. Right.

(Introductory questions to task)

Now, I want you to look at the sheet of paper I've given

	you. Look at the sheet of paper. Which train is described there? Which train?
Students	Bangalore Mail.
Teacher	Bangalore Mail. Where does it go?
Students	Bangalore.
Teacher	Bangalore. From where?
Students	Madras.
Teacher	From Madras. Is it a day train or a night train?
Students	Day . . . night train.
Teacher	It's a night train. How do you know? (*indicates student 3*)
Student 3	It's twenty-one forty.
Teacher	It starts at twenty-one forty. Twenty-one forty is . . .
Student	Nine . . .
Student	Eleven forty.
Teacher	Nine, not eleven. Nine forty . . . a.m. or p.m.?
Students	a.m. . . . p.m.
Teacher	p.m. yes, p.m. That's right. It's a night train . . . . (*pause*) Is the Brindavan a night train or a day train?
Student	Night . . .
Teacher	Is the Brindavan a night train or a day train?
Students	Day train.
Teacher	It's a day train. Is it a morning train or an afternoon train?
Students	Afternoon train.
Teacher	Afternoon train.
Students	Morning train.
Teacher	Who says afternoon train? One, two, three, four, five . . . uh who says morning train? . . . A lot of people. Yes, it's a morning train. It's true it arrives in Bangalore at one p.m. in the afternoon, but it starts at seven twenty-five a.m. early in the morning . . . um — morning train.

Appendix IVb

Transcript of the pre-task stages of a project lesson taught on 2 February 1983 to a class of ten-year-old children who were beginners in English and had had about ninety lessons on the project. The transcript was made by Esther Ramani.

(Preliminary pre-task)

Teacher	We are going to do another lesson today on timetables. OK? (*The teacher draws the columns and rows of a class timetable on the blackboard. At the head of the first column, she writes '9.30–10.15', the duration of the first period.*) What should I write here? (*pointing to the second column*)
Students	Ten fifteen – ten fifteen – ten fifteen.
Teacher	Ten fifteen.
Students	Eleven o'clock.
Teacher	Eleven o'clock. Here? (*pointing to the third column*)
Students	Eleven o'clock to eleven forty-five. (*tentative*)
Teacher	Eleven to . . . ?
Students	Eleven forty-five.
Teacher	Eleven to eleven forty-five.
Students	Eleven forty-five to (*not clear*)
Teacher	To?
Students	Twelve o'clock – twelve thirty – twelve thirty. (*many voices*)
Teacher	Twelve thirty. This is lunch, lunch break. And after lunch . . .
Students	Two o'clock. (*chorus*)
Teacher	Yes?
Students	Two forty-five. (*many voices*)
Teacher	Two forty-five. And the last period?
Students	Two forty-five to three thirty – three thirty – three forty-five – three thirty. (*several voices*)
Teacher	Three thirty. Yes. Who will write the names of the weekdays here? Who will write? (*Some students raise their hands. The teacher calls on one.*) Come. (*The

student writes the names of all the weekdays, Monday to
Friday correctly, the rest of class helping with the
spelling.) Is that correct?

Students   Correct.
Teacher   Right?
Students   Right.
Teacher   What about Saturday? Do they have school on Saturday?
Students   No . . . holiday.
Teacher   Holiday. Yes. It's a holiday on Saturday.

(Pre-task)

Now, the first period on Wednesday for this class, VI-B,
the first period on Wednesday is English. Who will come
and write that? (*Some students raise their hands. The*
teacher calls on one.) Yes, come. (*The student writes*
'*english*' *in the first period for Monday.*)

Students   Teacher – teacher! (*making a bid to correct*)
Teacher   Is that right?
Students   No – wrong. . . . Teacher – teacher!
Teacher   The first period on *Wednesday* is English.
           (*The student re-writes* '*english*' *in the right slot.*)
           Is this correct?
Students   Correct.
Teacher   This is correct. . . . You have to make a capital, big E.
           (*The student corrects the mistake.*)

Teacher   The second period on Tuesday is for Kannada. Who will
           write that? The second period on Tuesday is for
           Kannada. Yes? (*A student writes the correct answer on*
           the board.) Good.

Teacher   The last period on Thursday is for Games. . . . The last
           period on Thursday is for Games. Who will do that?
           Who will write that? (*A student comes up.*) The last
           period on Thursday is for Games. Yes? (*Peer consultation*
           is followed by the student writing '*G-o-m-e-s*' *in the last*
           period for Thursday morning.)

Teacher   Yes?
Students   Wrong – wrong.
Teacher   What is wrong?
Student   G-a-
Teacher   G-a. The spelling is wrong. OK. Change the spelling. G-
           a-m-e-s. (*The student corrects the spelling, but the entry*
           is still in the wrong slot.) Is that correct? Listen to my

	question. The *last* period on Thursday is for Games.
Students	Teacher – teacher!
Teacher	Yes, Shyambai. Yes, come along. (*Shyambai writes 'Games' in the right slot.*) Is that correct?
Students	Yes. Correct.
Teacher	How many say that this is correct? How many say this is correct? (*Some students raise their hands.*) You say this is correct . . . Yes? The last period on Thursday is for Games, that is from two forty-five to three thirty. You say *that* is correct. (*The teacher points to the second student's answer on the board.*) How many say eleven forty-five to twelve thirty is Games . . . *that* is correct. (*The teacher points to the first student's entry.*) How many children say that is correct? (*silence*) You don't understand? We have two answers here, right? Thursday eleven forty-five to twelve thirty . . . Games; Thursday two forty-five to three thirty . . . Games. Which is correct?
Students	Two forty-five to three thirty.
Teacher	How many say that is correct? How many of you say that is correct? (*The majority of hands go up.*) Why?
Student	Last period. (*very faint*)
Teacher	Did you listen to my question? I said the *last* period on Thursday is for Games. Which is the last period? Which is the last period?
Students	Two forty-five to three thirty.
Teacher	The last period of the *morning* is eleven forty-five to twelve thirty. Correct? The last period in the morning. Four periods in the morning . . . last period in the morning is eleven forty-five to twelve thirty. What I said was the *last* period, which is the last period for the day, for Thursday, so this is the right answer. (*The teacher erases the wrong answer.*)
Teacher	There is a Kannada lesson, there is a Kannada lesson in the first period on Monday.
Students	Teacher – teacher! (*A student comes up and writes the answer on the board with others calling out the spelling when needed.*)
Teacher	On Thursday – listen – on Thursday, there is a Maths lesson just before Games. On Thursday, there is a Maths lesson just before Games. Who will do that? Yes? (*tentative voices: A student comes up, and writes 'maths'.*)

Student	Big 'M'.
Teacher	What did you say?
Student	Big 'M'.
Teacher	Big 'M'. Yes. . . . Is that correct?
Students	Correct.
Teacher	On Friday, on Friday the period just before lunch is for History. On Friday, the period just before lunch is for History. (*silence*) On Friday, the period before lunch – just before lunch – is for History. (*There is peer discussion then one student puts up his hand.*)
Teacher	Nobody can do it, except Mubarak? Yes, come. (*The teacher calls on another student who has tentatively volunteered. He writes 'H-i-s-t-e-r-i' in the slot after lunch.*) All right?
Students	Spelling.
Teacher	Yes. The spelling is not correct. You know the spelling of History? Tell him.
Students	H-i-s-t-o-r-y.
Teacher	That's the spelling of History. (*The student corrects the spelling.*) Now is that correct, Mubarak?
Mubarak	No, wrong. (*faint*)
Teacher	Is that correct or wrong?
Students	Wrong.
Teacher	Wrong. Now where should you write History?
Students	Teacher – teacher!
Teacher	Yes, come. (*Another student comes up and writes 'History' in the right slot.*) Is that correct, Mubarak?
Students	Correct.
Teacher	Correct? What did I say? D'you remember what I said?
Mubarak	Before lunch. (*faint*)
Teacher	Yes – before – before what?
Students	Before lunch.
Teacher	Before lunch, just before lunch. Which is the period before lunch? Tell me the time.
Students	Two o'clock . . . eleven forty-five, eleven forty-five to twelve thirty. (*chorus*)
Teacher	That is the period just before lunch. This is lunch, isn't it? So the period just before lunch is . . .
Students	Eleven forty-five. (*chorus*)
Teacher	And I said . . . on Friday, the period just before lunch is for History. So this is correct. (*The teacher erases the wrong answer.*)

Teacher	The Science lesson, the Science lesson on Friday is just before History. The Science lesson on Friday is just before History. Who will do that? Yes? (*A student comes up and writes 's-c-i-n-s'*.)
Teacher	Is that all right? Yes?
Student	Wrong.
Teacher	What is wrong?
Student	Spelling.
Teacher	The spelling is wrong. OK. Who can give me the right spelling? Who can give him the right spelling? Stand up and say the right spelling.
Student	S-c-i-n . . .
Teacher	S-c-i . . .
Student	S-c-i-n . . .
Teacher	No. – *e*-n-c-e, S-c-i-e-n-c-e. Yes, Science. (*The student corrects the spelling, but begins the word with a small 's'*.)
Student	Big 'S'.
Teacher	Yes. . . . Yes. Good.
Teacher	The next question – listen – The first period after lunch on Tuesday is Geography. The first period after lunch on Tuesday is Geography. (*peer talk: No hands go up*.)
	Do you understand the question? Shall I say it again? Shall I repeat it? The first period after lunch on Tuesday is Geography. Yes? Want to try? (*Mubarak puts up his hand*.) Come, Mubarak. (*Mubarak comes to the board, locates the correct slot, but doesn't start writing. The teacher infers that the problem is spelling*.) I'll tell you the spelling. G-e-o . . . G-e-o-g-r-a-p-h-y. What is the— What— What time is the first period after lunch?
Students	Two o'clock. (*several voices*)
Teacher	Two o'clock to . . .?
Students	Two forty-five.
Teacher	Two to two forty-five. That's what I said. The first period after lunch on Tuesday. So that's right. Geography. Good.
Teacher	Next question. On Thursday the class is doing Science at ten thirty. On Thursday the class is doing Science at ten thirty. (*Several hands go up. The teacher selects one student, who writes the word in the right slot, but spells it wrong*.) Yes. The place is correct.
Students	Spelling, wrong – wrong.

Teacher	Wrongly spelt.
Students	– e – e.
Teacher	Good. I said the class is doing Science at ten thirty. In which period does ten thirty come? Which period?
Student	Two – two period.
Teacher	Second period. Yes, ten fifteen to eleven. So at ten thirty, I said they are doing Science. So, it's the second period. This is correct.
Teacher	Next question. At two thirty on Monday, at two thirty on Monday, the class is doing Hindi. The class is doing Hindi at two thirty on Monday. Yes? (*A student comes up and writes the correct answer.*) Is that right?
Students	Right. Correct.
Teacher	Is that right?
Students	Yes.
Teacher	Yes. Which period is that?
Students	First period.
Teacher	First period . . .
Student	After lunch.
Teacher	After lunch. Yes – first period after lunch. And what is the timing?
Students	Two o'clock. (*several voices*)
Teacher	Yes. Two o'clock to two forty-five. So two thirty is the first period after lunch; so that's the right answer.
Teacher	Now listen to the next question. In the third period of the morning, in the third period of the morning on Tuesday, the class is doing English.
Students	Teacher – teacher! (*A student comes up and writes the correct answer.*)
Teacher	Is that right?
Students	Right. Correct.
Teacher	Correct? All of you say it's correct?
Students	Correct.
Teacher	That is the third period in the morning. Now, this is the last question before you write. . . . This is the last question before you write. The last periods on Wednesday and Friday are for Drawing. The last periods on Wednesday and Friday are for Drawing. (*peer talk: Some hands go up.*) Yes? (*A student comes up and writes 'D-o-r-i-n-g' in the slot for Wednesday.*) Is that right?
Students	Wrong – wrong.
Teacher	What is wrong?

Student	The spelling.
Teacher	The spelling. The spelling is wrong. Can you give him the right spelling? Yes?
Student	D-r-o-w-i-n-g.
Teacher	Is that the right spelling? Yes?
Student	D-r-a-w-i-n-g.
Teacher	Yes – D-r-*a*-w-i-n-g. (*The student at the board corrects the spelling and starts to go back to his place.*) Has he finished?
Students	Finished . . . Friday – Friday!
Teacher	Friday. (*The student returns to the board and writes 'Drawing' in the slot for Friday as well.*) Is that right? Is that correct?
Students	Correct.
Teacher	Yes. The last period. That's the last period – On Wednesday and Friday – is for . . .
Students	Drawing.
Teacher	Now here there are some blank timetables. Take one and pass the rest. (*The timetables are distributed.*) Have you all got one?

The task stage of the lesson consists of similar instructions from the teacher for completing a blank timetable, listened to and carried out by students individually.

Appendix V
List of task-types used on the project

1 Diagrams and formations

a Naming parts of a diagram with numbers and letters of the alphabet, as instructed.

b Placing numbers and letters of the alphabet in relation to one another, as instructed, to arrive at particular formations.

c Placing numbers and letters of the alphabet in given crossword formats; constructing/completing such formats, as instructed.

2 Drawing

a Drawing geometrical figures/formations from sets of verbal instructions.

b Formulating verbal instructions for drawing/completing such figures.

c Comparing given figures to identify similarities and differences.

3 Clockfaces

a Telling the time from a clockface; positioning the hands of a clock to show a given time.

b Calculating durations from the movement of a clock's hands; working out intervals between given times.

c Stating the time on a twelve hour clock and a twenty-four hour clock; relating times to phases of the day and night.

4 Monthly calendars

a Relating dates to days of the week.

b Calculating durations in days and weeks (in the context of travel, leave, etc).

c Identifying relevant dates or days of the week in relation to cyclic activity (e.g. 'twice a week').

5 Maps

a Finding, naming, or describing specific locations on a given map.

b Constructing/completing a map from given descriptions/ instructions.

c Constructing the floor-plan of a house from a description.

d Deciding on the best route from one place to another; giving directions.

e Deciding on the best form of transport (given information on bus routes, fares, etc).

f Making decisions on good/bad siting (e.g. of a new hospital or school).

6 School timetables

a Constructing class timetables from instructions/descriptions.

b Comparing such timetables to identify the frequencies of lessons in different subjects (or possibilities for different students to exchange shared materials, etc).

c Constructing timetables for teachers of particular subjects from given class timetables, and vice versa.

7 Programmes and itineraries

a Interpreting individuals' daily routines (e.g. to say where a person is at a given time).

b Relating the routines of different individuals (e.g. members of a family) to tell who is where at given times, etc.

c Constructing itemized programmes from narrative accounts (involving a re-ordering of events and/or some inference).

d Inferring where something must have happened (e.g. something lost/left behind) from a narrative account of activities.

e Constructing itineraries from descriptions of travel or from a statement of needs and intentions.

f Working out feasible timings for personal appointments (e.g. going to the bank, meeting a friend) consistent with the requirements of work, travel, etc.

8 *Train timetables*

a Interpreting train timetables (i.e. identifying arrival and departure times, stopping places, and durations).

b Constructing train timetables from given descriptions of travel.

c Selecting trains appropriate to given needs/intentions; making travel plans.

d Working out the consequences of a train's delay at a given place for arrivals/departures at other places, for onward travel by other trains, etc.

e Filling in forms for making/cancelling train reservations; composing messages to request onward reservations, and to convey arrival times, etc.

9 *Age and year of birth*

a Working out year of birth from age, and vice versa.

b Inferring who is younger/older, how old, when born, etc. from general descriptions of families or peer-groups.

c Relating individuals' age/year of birth to given age requirements (e.g. for school enrolment, driving, voting).

10 *Money*

a Working out the money needed to buy a set of things (e.g. school stationery, vegetables) from given price lists and needs.

b Deciding on quantities to be bought with the money available; inferring quantities bought from the money spent.

c Discovering errors in bills; inferring when an underpayment/ overpayment must have taken place.

d Deciding between alternatives in shopping (e.g. between a small store nearby and a large one which involves lower prices but expenditure on transport).

e Working out possibilities of saving, from information about incomes and expenses.

11 *Tabular information*

a Interpreting information presented in tables – e.g. about

books (columns for title, author, publisher, price, year of publication); applicants for a job (columns for age, qualifications, past employment); also schools, hotels, etc.

b Constructing such tables from given descriptions.

c Deciding on choices (e.g. of a school for a given child) which best meet given needs.

d Making generalizations from tables; testing generalizations against them.

12 Distances

a Working out the distances between places, from given distances between other places or from the scale of a map.

b Comparing distances and deciding on desirable routes of travel in given situations.

c Constructing maps from distances and directions inferred from given descriptions.

13 Rules

a Interpreting sets of rules, e.g. those for concessional bus tickets for students; railway concessions for holiday travel; a savings account in a bank; membership of a library.

b Applying rules to given cases/situations; examining the consequences of a breach, and deciding on the best course of action.

c Identifying anomalies/problems in rules and deciding on desirable amendments.

14 The postal system

a Interpreting the Postal Index Number code (prevalent in India) from a given description; relating the numbering system to a map of India.

b Inferring the geographical location of places from their postal code numbers; determining, from such numbers, the relative distance/proximity between different places.

c Working out the postal code numbers for particular places from geographical information and/or from the numbers for other places.

d Identifying errors in the writing of the postal code in

particular instances and possible consequences for the transmission of the letters concerned.

e Identifying the advantages/difficulties of the postal code system and deciding on possible improvements.

f Interpreting the related system of Quick Mail Service and determining its relevance in given cases.

g Deciding on the quickest way to send a letter, given a set of circumstances and the rules of Quick Mail Service.

15 *Telegrams*

a Interpreting given telegrams in relation to their context (e.g. deciding between alternative interpretations, identifying possible misinterpretations.)

b Composing telegrams for given purposes, with the aim of reconciling economy with clarity.

c Discovering errors made in the drafting or transmission of telegrams, from given accounts of events/actions.

16 *Stories and dialogues*

a Listening to stories (of a 'whodunit' kind) and completing them with appropriate solutions.

b Reading stories or dialogues and answering comprehension questions (particularly of an inferential kind) on them.

c Completing or continuing given dialogues, as appropriate to given situations.

d Identifying factual inconsistencies in given narrative or descriptive accounts.

17 *Classification*

a Finding the 'odd man out' in a given set of objects or a classified list.

b Making classified lists from unclassified ones.

c Deciding on classifications suited to given purposes.

18 *Personal details*

a Finding items of information relevant to a particular situation in an individual's curriculum vitae.

b Constructing a curriculum vitae from personal descriptions.

c Organizing/reorganizing a curriculum vitae for a given purpose/audience.

d Working out ways of tracing the owners of objects, from information gathered from the objects.

Appendix VI
Evaluation of the Bangalore Project

Alan Beretta and Alan Davies

Published in the *ELT Journal*, Volume 39/2, April 1985.

The Bangalore/Madras Communicational Teaching Project (CTP) was the subject of a searching discussion by Brumfit in an earlier issue of this Journal [Brumfit 1984b]. The present article may be seen as a follow up to that discussion. The main purpose here is to disseminate the results of an independent evaluation of the CTP that was carried out early in 1984. Firstly, a brief account is given of the aims and principles of the CTP itself. Following this, some of the problems involved in the evaluation are considered, and the adopted framework, tests, and hypotheses are described. Finally, the results are discussed and appropriate conclusions drawn.

The CTP: a brief description

Our description of the Bangalore/Madras Communicational Teaching Project (CTP) need only be brief, as the principles and methodology have already been documented more fully in the published sources. (The most accessible are Brumfit 1984a, Brumfit 1984b, and Johnson 1982.) The CTP grew out of a dissatisfaction with 'structural' teaching. Notional/functional syllabuses were considered, but Dr Prabhu[1] and his associates believed that the need for a change in syllabus content was less pressing than the need for a change in methodology. This belief was fuelled by the expectation that linguists' generalizations about language structure are unlikely to match whatever generalizations are involved in the learner's process of grammar construction. Thus, the CTP syllabus contains no linguistic specification at all, but instead comprises a series of tasks in the form of problem-solving activities. The central tenet of the CTP is that language form is best learnt when the learner's attention is focused on meaning. More specifically,

Grammar-construction by the learner is an unconscious process which is best facilitated by bringing about in the learner a preoccupation with meaning, saying or doing. (*Prabhu 1982:2*)

Consequently, the syllabus is dictated by the methodology, which is three-pronged: pre-task, task, and feedback. The 'pre-task' makes known the nature of the task, brings relevant language into play, regulates the difficulty level of the task, and allows some learners to learn from attempts made by others. The task itself is a period of self-reliant effort by each learner to achieve a clearly perceived goal (e.g. interpreting a schedule or a map). The 'feedback' gives the learners an indication of how successfully they have done the task.

Difficulties in evaluating the CTP

The stated purpose in seeking an evaluation was:

to assess, through appropriate tests, whether there is any demonstrable difference in terms of attainment in English between classes of children who have been taught on the CTP and their peers who have received normal instruction in the respective schools. (*Prabhu 1983: personal communication*)

The second author of the present article was invited to report on the feasibility of an evaluation during a visit to South India in 1983. As a result of his report, which provided a design for the evaluation, the first author constructed the 'instruments' and visited India to carry out the evaluation in early 1984.

Our brief was to compare the communicational method with the Indian version of the structural method. Comparisons of methods, as an approach to evaluation, have an undistinguished history in language teaching research. Most notably, the attempts by Scherer and Wertheimer (1964) and Smith (1970) to compare the audio-lingual method with the cognitive code failed to yield conclusive results. But, as Stern remarks,

The inconclusiveness of these studies does not mean that research is a waste of time. The studies gradually revealed that the 'methods' are not clearly defined entities that can be juxtaposed and compared. It would be a waste of time if that lesson had not been learnt. (*Stern 1983:71*)

On the other hand, Krashen argues that some methods, for example Total Physical Response,[2] have been shown to be 'superior to others' (Krashen 1982:155–60). This type of comparison implies that we can make a distinction between some methods and others, or between one method and another. But things are not so simple. Methods are notoriously difficult to pin down. 'Method' may imply a particular syllabus content (for example, a selection and arrangement of structures or functions); or it may involve certain set classroom practices (as with the Silent Way[3]), or both. Any one method may have a variety of manifestations, some of which may be barely distinguishable from the methods they are to be contrasted with. This is illustrated in Valette's comment about the distinctions between certain teaching methods:

> . . . the features which the modified traditional and the modified audio-lingual [methods] have in common are more numerous than those which divide them. (*Valette 1969:397*)

Although we would not wish to endorse global comparisons, there seem to be reasonable grounds to believe that the CTP is sufficiently distinct from the structural method to avoid ambiguity or overlap.

Given our brief, there were two major problems facing us: firstly, how to control the investigation in a way that would be experimentally valid; and secondly, how to produce tests that would be equally fair to both teaching methods.

Experimental control

The evaluation design assumed two types of class: CTP classes were to be regarded as 'experimental', and structural classes as 'control'. A true experiment would require students to be randomly assigned to experimental and control classes, so as to ensure initial equivalence of the two groups. However, since the CTP was not set up in this way, it was necessary to adopt a less rigorous design which involved intact classes.[4] Thus, caution is required when assessing the validity of the experiment.

Basically, the problem concerns the conflicting demands of 'internal' and 'external' validity. Internal validity has to do with factors which may directly affect test scores, while external validity is concerned with generalizability. If all variables, such as the school environment, the selection of groups, the age and social background of learners, and so on, are strictly controlled, then we might say that 'laboratory conditions' pertain, and that the evaluation is internally valid. However, what occurs under such conditions may *not* occur in normal circumstances, and the question arises: how far may we generalize from the results? By contrast, if the experiment is carried out in real school settings, this may facilitate generalizability and make the evaluation more valid externally, but the reliability of the data can then be questioned. For example, perhaps one group of learners managed better results than another because they were more advanced to start with, or because they had greater motivation.

The study

Four schools, each with one 'experimental' and one 'control' class were included in the evaluation (see *Table a*). In evaluating the CTP, the most serious threat to internal validity was that in one of the schools (T. Nagar), one group had maintained its stability over a period of time while the other had not. In addition, in the same school a third of the students in one group were not available for our tests. As for external validity, three of the four experimental groups were taught by better qualified, more highly motivated teachers, and in addition they were frequently observed and were consequently aware of being 'guinea pigs'. Given the origins and evolution of the CTP – the idea was generated by a few people, and tried out in circumstances which were far from ideal and accompanied by openness to public scrutiny – most of these problems were unavoidable. Nevertheless, the threats to validity must be stated clearly, as they have implications for the interpretation of the results.

Test content bias

It was clear that if we used tests that were solely CTP-based, we would be unfair to the structural group, and vice versa. The problem is a familiar one in educational research. A review of twenty-six studies which attempted to compare curricula concluded that

. . . innovative students do better when the criterion is well matched to the innovative curriculum, and traditional students do better when the criterion is matched to the traditional curriculum. (*Walker and Schaffarzick 1974:94*)

Although there is no neat, conclusive remedy to this problem, some investigators have tried to overcome 'test content bias' by using achievement tests, one favouring each method. Others have tried to develop tests that focus on areas of proficiency and reflect patterns of emphasis. For our purposes, we decided to construct a battery of tests intended to measure *achievement* separately for experimental and control groups (by a structure test and a CTP task-based test), and *proficiency* by three 'neutral' measures: contextualized grammar, dictation, and listening/reading comprehension.

Description of the tests [5]

The achievement tests were designed as measures of each method, while the proficiency tests required some degree of transfer from classroom practice. With reference to tests of contextualized grammar, Krashen and Terrell comment:

> While it is possible that the student will understand the meaning and fill in the blank on the basis of acquired knowledge, it is also possible that the student will simply figure out the morphological pattern . . . without even understanding the text. (*Krashen and Terrell 1983:167*)

If this is true, then both CTP and structural classes would be equally advantaged or equally disadvantaged on a test of this nature.

Our justification for dictation tests rests on the theory proposed by Oller (1979 and elsewhere) that dictation tests measure a learner's 'grammar of expectancy'. He maintains that if the segments are too long to be memorized and regurgitated, they must be reconstituted by drawing on the grammar of expectancy. Performance is therefore more or less successful, depending on the sophistication of the learner's grammatical competence. Dictation may also be regarded as a sentence-bound test, thereby measuring structural awareness. In either case, dictation seemed to be a test suitable both to experimental and to control groups.

The listening/reading comprehension test is one of receptive ability to use language. Its function was to determine how far what is learnt in structural and CTP classrooms can be deployed.

Hypotheses

Three hypotheses were to be confirmed or disconfirmed by the results of the above tests:

1 there is a difference between the language abilities arising from form-focused teaching and those arising from meaning-focused teaching. Thus, we expected each group to perform significantly better on its own achievement test;

2 acquisition of non-syllabus-based structure is best achieved without focus on form; if this were true, experimental classes would do significantly better than control classes on the proficiency tests of contextualized grammar and dictation;

3 structure acquired *without* focus on form is more readily available for deployment than structure learned *with* focus on form; for this to be confirmed, CTP groups would have to score significantly higher than control groups on the proficiency test of listening/reading comprehension.

Results

The results of the tests in the four schools are summarized in *Table a.*[6] We have mentioned that the difficulties of appropriate test construction and of controlling experimental variables would modify interpretation of results. However, *Table a* does offer some vindication of the tests themselves. The superior knowledge of the experimental and control groups on the two tests designed as measures of the two methods indicates that the two measures do assess different kinds of learning. As for the proficiency tests, the experimental groups do better in five out of twelve possible results, and in no case does the control group do better. This ragged pattern suggests that the tests are reasonably unbiased and that they allow for legitimate competition between the two groups.

Controlling experimental variables was always going to be difficult, since the project was not organized with such an evaluation in mind. Nevertheless, from the limited information available (results in other subjects, and headmasters' and teachers' judgements), there is some reason to believe that the groups were initially equivalent, even though not randomly constituted. However, the serious threat to internal validity mentioned above makes it very difficult to interpret the T. Nagar results, and consequently, we ignore them as confirmation or rejection of hypotheses.

In the other three schools, as can be seen from *Table a*, both the experimental and the control groups did significantly better on their own achievement tests, satisfying the demands of the first hypothesis. The requirements of the third hypothesis are also fulfilled, as the experimental groups significantly outperformed control groups on the test of listening/reading comprehension. The second hypothesis, that acquisition of non-syllabus-based structure is best achieved without focus on form, is partly borne out. There was no significant difference in two of the schools on the dictation and contextualized

Table a   *Group means and patterns of significance for four schools and five tests*

School	Group	Structure		Contextualized grammar		Dictation		Listening/reading comprehension		Task-based	
		Class mean	*p = 5%	Class mean	*p = 5%	Class mean	*p = 5%	Class mean	*p = 5%	Class mean	*p = 5%
Ba	C	10·27	'C'	8·17	'='	15·11	'E'	9·20	'E'	12·02	'E'
	E	8·07		9·76		18·67		18·26		19·26	
Cu	C	8·31	'C'	3·38	'E'	8·79	'='	3·52	'E'	3·39	'E'
	E	4·53		6·03		11·38		18·03		6·76	
T.Na	C	8·63	'C'	5·64	'='	14·6	'='	10·03	'='	9·31	'E'
	E	5·15		4·32		11·7		7·65		14·00	
Ti	C	10·07	'C'	6·11	'='	18·34	'='	11·26	'E'	11·21	'E'
	E	8·41		5·55		19·29		14·73		13·74	

The four schools were at Jayanagar, Bangalore (Ba), Cuddalore (Cu), T. Nagar (T.Na), and Tiruvottiyur (Ti).

*p = 5 per cent means that for the two-tail 't' test used, the 5 per cent level was selected to determine significance, i.e. t at the ·05 level of significance.

In the column headed 'p = 5 per cent', 'E' indicates that the experimental group did significantly better, '=' that there was no significant difference, and 'C' that the control group did significantly better.

grammar tests, but in the Bangalore school the experimental pupils did significantly better on the dictation, as they did in the Cuddalore school on the contextualized grammar test.

In short, the results reveal a pattern which is consistent with the first and third hypotheses, and in part consistent with the second (and central) hypothesis.

Conclusion

From the beginning, it was our view that the results of the evaluation might constitute a 'probe' of the central CTP hypothesis, but not 'proof'. The impossibility of full experimental control, and the potential for bias in test construction make generalization impossible. Also, the fact that no group of learners has been exposed to the CTP treatment for more than three years precludes any firm statement about the effectiveness of this method at later stages of learning. While admitting these limitations, we regard the results as being, on the whole, positive and conclude that they provide tentative support for the CTP claim that grammar construction can take place through a focus on meaning alone.[7]

Notes

1 Dr N. S. Prabhu (then) of the British Council, Madras, initiated the project in 1979, and directed its activities throughout.

2 Total Physical Response is the name of a method given prominence by J. Asher (e.g. in his article 'The total physical approach to second language learning' in *Modern Language Journal* 53:3–17). It involves a lengthy period of listening to and carrying out instructions in the foreign language.

3 See *ELT Journal* 36/4:237–41 for a discussion with Dr Gattegno, creator of the Silent Way.

4 For discussion of quasi-experimental designs, see Campbell and Stanley (1963).

5 For samples of the Tests see Appendix A.

6 This table is merely a broad summary. Those requiring further details should contact the authors.

7 We acknowledge our gratitude to all those in South India who made this evaluation such a rewarding experience for us. In particular we thank Dr Prabhu, his colleagues, and the teachers and pupils of the four schools.

References

Brumfit, C. J. 1984a. *Communicative Methodology in Language Teaching: the Roles of Fluency and Accuracy.* Cambridge: Cambridge University Press.

Brumfit, C. J. 1984b. 'The Bangalore Procedural Syllabus.' *ELT Journal* 38/4:233–41.

Campbell, D. T. and J. C. Stanley. 1963. 'Experimental and quasi-experimental designs for research on teaching' in N. L. Gage (ed.). 1963. *Handbook of Research on Teaching.* Chicago: Rand McNally.

Johnson, K. 1982. *Communicative Syllabus Design and Methodology.* Oxford: Pergamon.

Krashen, S. D. 1982. *Principles and Practice in Second Language Acquisition.* Oxford: Pergamon.

Krashen, S. D. and T. D. Terrell. 1983. *The Natural Approach: Language Acquisition in the Classroom.* Oxford: Pergamon/Alemany.

Oller, J. W. 1979. *Language Tests at School.* London: Longman.

Prabhu, N. S. 1982. 'The Communicational Teaching Project, South India.' Madras: The British Council (mimeo).

Scherer, G. and M. Wertheimer. 1964. *A Psycholinguistic Experiment in Foreign Language Teaching.* New York: McGraw Hill.

Smith, P. D. Jnr. 1970. *A Comparison of the Cognitive and Audio-Lingual Approaches to Foreign Language Instruction: The Pennsylvania Foreign Language Project.* Philadelphia: The Center for Curriculum Development.

Stern, H. H. 1983. *Fundamental Concepts of Language Teaching.* Oxford: Oxford University Press.

Valette, R. M. 1969. 'The Pennsylvania Project, its conclusions and its implications.' *Modern Language Journal* 53/6:396–404.

Walker, D. F. and J. Schaffarzick. 1974. 'Comparing curricula.' *Review of Educational Research* 44:83–111.

Appendix

The following five tests were used:

1 Structure
2 Contextualized grammar
3 Dictation
4 Listening/reading comprehension
5 Task-based

1 *Structure:* This test consisted of a series of multiple-choice items. The structures were drawn from the Karnataka and Tamil Nadu State syllabuses. Example:

We _____ going to school today. It's Sunday.
a aren't   **b** not   **c** isn't   **d** don't

2 *Contextualized grammar:* This comprised a number of items where the testee was required to fill in the blank with one word. Example:

Through the window I can see my father. He can't see me because he _____ looking at the road. He is going to the market.

3 *Dictation:* A short passage was dictated in the following way:

i reading of whole passage at conversational speed; e.g.

I have two brothers and three sisters. We all go to the same school. Sometimes we take the bus. Today we are going by bus. After school we will walk home.

ii one reading only of each segment at conversational speed;

iii final reading of whole passage at conversational speed.

4 *Listening/reading comprehension:* This required testees to read, for example, a hotel advertisement and to write answers to spoken questions. It demanded a great deal of inference; e.g.

Hotel Ashok: One room only Rs 150 a day! Bring your family! In our grounds you can enjoy cricket, football, and kabaddi. We have a good restaurant. English and Indian meals. Film show every night at 8 p.m. Write to: Hotel Ashok, 74 Gandhi Street, Delhi. Tel. 883921.

Listen carefully to the questions. You will hear each question twice. Answer the questions, using the information from the advertisement.

e.g. Spoken question: *Where is the hotel?*

5 *Task-based:* The test was a representative sample of the tasks used in the CTP classroom. For example, solving problems related to a timetable and to a calendar.